WHOLLY LIVING

JOHN A. HUFFMAN, JR.

WHOLLY LIVING

This book is designed for your personal reading pleasure and profit. It is also designed for group study. A 13-session Leader's Guide with helps and hints for teachers and visual aids (Victor Multiuse Transparency Masters) is available from your local bookstore or from the publisher.

R. Rosmullen
1-21-83

VICTOR BOOKS

a division of SP Publications, Inc.
WHEATON. ILLINOIS 60187

Offices also in Fullerton, California • Whitby, Ontario, Canada • Amersham-on-the-Hill, Bucks, England

Most of the Scripture quotations in this book are from the *New International Version* (NIV), © 1978 by the New York International Bible Society. Other quotations are from the *King James Version* (KJV) and *The New Testament in Modern English* (PH), © J. B. Phillips 1958, The Macmillan Company. Used by permission.

Recommended Dewey Decimal Classification: 227.6
Suggested Subject Headings: PHILIPPIANS: A CHRISTIAN LIFESTYLE

Library of Congress Catalog Card Number: 80-52948
ISBN: 0-89693-005-X

VICTOR BOOKS
A division of SP Publications, Inc.
P.O. Box 1825 • Wheaton, Illinois 60187

CONTENTS

1
Becoming a Complete Person

Being confident of this, that He who began a good work in you will carry it on to completion until the day of Christ Jesus.

It is right for me to feel this way about all of you, since I have you in my heart; for whether I am in chains or defending and confirming the Gospel, all of you share in God's grace with me. God can testify how I long for all of you with the affection of Christ Jesus.

And this is my prayer: that your love may abound more and more in knowledge and depth of insight, so that you may be able to discern what is best and may be pure and blameless until the day of Christ, filled with the fruit of righteousness that comes through Jesus Christ—to the glory and praise of God (Phil. 1:6-11).

Principles for confident living existed long before the introduction of Dale Carnegie courses or the proclamations of positive or possibility thinking by well-known preachers. The Apostle Paul, writing to Christians at Philippi, presented several excellent concepts for confident living. The study of this extraordinary letter to the Philippians will clarify more fully what God does in each believer. Paul wrote the letter to a church in northern Greece which he had helped start during his second missionary journey about A.D. 52.

Philippi was a strategic city made distinct by at least three characteristics: Because of gold and silver mines, which had been worked hundreds of years, it had become a commercial center. It was a Roman colony filled with people proud of their unique citizenship. The city itself had been founded in 368 B.C. by Philip II, father of Alexander the Great, at an important site commanding the road from Europe to Asia.

Paul and Silas had founded a church in Philippi. Paul wrote to this church 10 or 12 years later from his prison cell in Rome. He expressed thanks to his brothers and sisters in Christ who had been faithful in supporting him. He also encouraged them in their trials, and made a classic appeal for them to remember their unity in Jesus Christ.

Paul opened his letter with his typical words of encouragement. He wished them God's grace and peace. He expressed his enormous thanksgiving for the partnership he had shared with them in the Gospel of Jesus Christ, from the first day he had met with them to the present.

Then Paul targeted his message to believers, both at Philippi and today, with these words: "Being confident of this, that He who began a good work in you will carry it on to completion until the day of Christ Jesus" (v. 6). This verse involved the whole process of becoming a complete person in Christ.

Being Confident in God

A couple of years ago, two repairmen came to our house; one to fix the clothes dryer, the other to recharge an air conditioner. I immediately liked the first man. Pondering on it later, I realized that it was his approach that was pleasing. He appeared to know what he was doing; dismantling parts of the dryer, replacing two parts, and putting it all back together rather quickly. He had no doubt about what needed to be done.

The second repairman came to service the air conditioner. For six or seven weeks he worked on it at intermittent times. I began to lose confidence in him. He seemed sure of himself, but that wasn't enough. He finally admitted he really didn't know what was wrong and advised me to call someone else.

Paul expressed a different kind of confidence—confidence in God: "I always pray with joy . . . being confident of this, that He who began a good work in you will carry it on to completion until the day of Christ Jesus" (vv. 4-6). Paul's confidence was not placed in another human being or in himself, but in the Lord. How exciting to know the trustworthiness of the Lord which gives a person confidence. Take your eyes off Jesus Christ and you are in trouble. Lean on your money, prestige, power, or competence, and you will find that you are resting on glass crutches.

Are you looking to yourself or to others? Have you put your trust in the Lord? Can you say with the Psalmist David, "To You, O Lord, I lift up my soul; in You I trust, O my God"? (Ps. 25:1-2) Such confidence rests on God, and on absolutely nothing else. God is the active Agent. He is the Creator, the Sustainer. He gives substantial ground for confident living. Any other assurance is superficial.

Believers Have a Point of Beginning

You don't become a Christian by osmosis. God acts through His Holy Spirit, to bring you to repentance and trust in Jesus Christ. He is the Initiator. If you are a believer, there was a beginning point.

Paul was in a reflective mood. It had been over a decade since he had first encountered the people at Philippi and his mind filled with memories as he dictated those words, "He who began a good work in you . . ." (Phil. 1:6). He could remember those early converts who made up the nucleus of believers at Philippi. God had touched their lives! There was Lydia, the rich lady from Thyatira, whom he had met by the little river Ganga outside Philippi. She had a business selling purple goods. He and Silas had told her about Jesus. The Lord had opened her heart to hear the Good News. She had put her trust in the Saviour and had been baptized, along with others of her household. God had taken action, changed her life, and had begun His good work in her.

Paul could remember how, on that same day, God had begun a good work in a fortune-telling slave girl from whom an evil spirit was exorcised. God was at work, putting His action into the lives of people.

Paul also remembered how God's action on behalf of that little girl had caused him to be thrown into jail. The masters who owned her had dragged Paul and Silas before the magistrates and had charged them with disturbing the peace. After all, the opponents had lost their source of diabolical livelihood through God's action as revealed in Paul and Silas.

In jail, God again began another good work by literally shaking the foundations of the prison. This led to the conversion of the Philippian jailer and his family.

Paul remembered these changed lives as he thought back to the beginnings of that church at Philippi. How many more, whom he knew personally, had come to trust the Saviour? How many more had experienced God's work in their lives? Now, years later, what would he say to them? What could he say to them? So many experiences, joys and sorrows had intervened. Yes, there was the beginning, that divine action of regeneration in which lives were born into the kingdom of God.

If you are a member of God's family, yours may not have been a highly emotional beginning. But there came a point at which your life opened to God's action. In your own way you said yes to what God had done in Jesus Christ. Dietrich Bonhoeffer stated the necessity for a definite beginning: "Unless a definite step is demanded, the call vanishes into thin air; and if men imagine that they can follow Jesus without taking this step, they are deluding themselves" (*The Cost of Discipleship,* Macmillan, p. 53). John Stott points out the difference between this specific opening of oneself and mere religious activities when he says:

> This step is the beginning and nothing else will do instead.
> You can believe in Christ intellectually and admire Him;
> you can say your prayers to Him through the keyhole (as I
> did for many years); you can push coins at Him under the
> door; you can be moral, decent, upright and good; you
> can be religious and pious; you can have been baptized
> and confirmed; you can be deeply versed in the philos-
> ophy of religion; you can be a theological student and
> even an ordained minister—and still not have opened the

door to Jesus Christ. There is no substitute for this (*Basic Christianity*, InterVarsity Press, p. 127).

Still in Process

Your salvation is accomplished, it is secure. But you are still in process. You have not fully arrived. This good work is an ongoing function of God's Spirit. You are in the process of becoming complete. You are not yet complete. This good work is a work of sanctification, a work which is not finished in a single blow, but is carried forward through gradual development. Yours is a "pilgrim's progress," moving through various circumstances of life, accompanied by the Lord.

I find it quite exciting to know that I'm in process—to know that God is accomplishing His good work in me now. Frankly, if what I could see in my spiritual mirror was the final product, I wouldn't be too happy. Would you? You and I are not as yet complete.

Self-righteousness is a malady you and I can get into when we forget that we are "in process." Do you fight the battle of thinking more of yourself than you ought to? And then do you plunge from a high of self-confidence to a low of despair? I do. How much I want to do what I should. How I desire to be an authentic servant of the Lord. Then I fail. I say things I shouldn't. I become judgmental, taking prerogatives which belong only to the Lord. I talk about another person behind his back. My tongue so quickly fulfills James' description: "The tongue is also a fire . . . it sets the whole course of his life on fire" (James 3:6).

"But where sin abounded, grace did much more abound" (Rom. 5:20, KJV). There is cleansing, forgiveness, and refreshment in coming to the Lord. "If we confess our sins, He is faithful and just and will forgive us our sins and purify us from all unrighteousness" (1 John 1:9). But this isn't a once-and-for-all act. Graciously, God is bringing us along the road of Christian maturity which can be likened to the physical process of growth from infancy to adulthood. This continuing process is one in which the Holy Spirit is present, working to His glory.

Keith Miller shows us this process in his book *The Becomers*

(Word Books, p. 11). He writes about an exciting brand of Christian who has begun with Christ in Christian commitment, and now, in the growth process is open and vulnerable to the work of the Holy Spirit. This kind of Christian sees "that conversion is only a beginning and not an arrival. The convert has just been freed to start actualizing the gifts and potentialities which have always been inherent in his life. He thinks of himself as a 'becomer' in the process."

God Is Completing His Work in Us

There's good news for us if we get a bit concerned about our spiritual development. Paul writes: "He who began a good work in you will carry it on to completion until the day of Christ Jesus" (Phil. 1:6).

There is a sense in which we must trust the Lord even when we begin to doubt His promises or the circumstances of life which bombard us. When we have many problems or we no longer have the same excitement which was once ours spiritually, we need to rest in the assurance that God, who is leading us step by step through the maturing process, knows the end to it all. The day will come when we will be complete. We will be perfect in the day of Jesus Christ when we step into His presence.

Our God has sufficient means to complete that good work which He has already begun in us. To suggest that He can't is an insult to His infinite abilities. An unfinished project is an insult to a builder. God has the total capacity to finish every good work He has begun. If we look beyond ourselves, we can be confident that He is carrying out His lifelong processes and is fully capable of bringing them to completion.

God's Work Abounds through Prayer

One of the best ways to strip away wrong attitudes toward another person is to pray for that person. In the process of praying we extricate ourselves from petty irritations which destroy relationships, and achieve perspective on what is best for that person. Positive prayer helps us see another as God sees him. It enables us to wish him the best, and then begin to see that best accomplished in his life.

Prayer was that connective element which held Paul in communication with the believers at Philippi, and denied the distance of years and miles. Paul not only prayed for his friends, but he also wrote to them as well, and told them how he prayed. Inspired by the Holy Spirit, he communicated what God wanted to do in them.

A careful look at Paul's prayer for his believing friends (vv. 9-11) alerts us to what God wants to accomplish in us. This prayer gives a specific definition of some crucial elements in the process of becoming complete persons in Christ.

Increase Your Capacity to Love

We know we ought to love. How many times have we read 1 Corinthians 13, only to feel guilty? It's frustrating, isn't it? In the opening verses, Paul blasts away at those who mistake gifts, theological brilliance, unlimited faith, and acts of humanitarianism as true Christianity. Instead, he moves beyond these good actions of Christian living to the attitudinal level, setting a standard which seems impossible:

> This love of which I speak is slow to lose patience—it looks for a way of being constructive. It is not possessive: it is neither anxious to impress nor does it cherish inflated ideas of its own importance.
>
> Love has good manners and does not pursue selfish advantage. It is not touchy. It does not compile statistics of evil or gloat over the wickedness of other people. On the contrary, it is glad with all good men when Truth prevails.
>
> Love knows no limit to its endurance, no end to its trust, no fading of its hope; it can outlast anything. It is, in fact, the one thing that still stands when all else has fallen (1 Cor. 13:4-7, PH).

Just reading that makes me feel guilty until I suddenly realize that Paul's prayer is that "love may abound more and more." We have not fully arrived in our capacity to love. This is an ongoing process of God's Holy Spirit which sensitizes us to what God wants accomplished in our lives. Love can grow, or love can be suppressed. In the process there can be a steady forward movement as our love for Him and our appreciation for His Word increases. So, instead of feeling guilty for our failures we can open our lives to the Lord as an expression of our love for Him.

Keeping Love on Track

Unfortunately, our society is flooded with much irresponsible loving. There's a difference between sentimentality, which makes a display of emotion, and deep authentic caring. Love is meant to be discerning. True Christian love is not "easy come, easy go." There is no place in the Christian faith for a happy-go-lucky acceptance of everyone and everything. The discerning Christian is not tossed about by every wind of doctrine. A responsible Christian does not accept all approaches and lifestyles as legitimate, irrespective of biblical norms.

Paul expresses two corrective qualities which keep true love on track. He writes, "And this is my prayer: that your love may abound more and more in knowledge and depth of insight" (Phil. 1:9).

The first quality is knowledge. A responsible, growing love is one which goes through a constant process of education. It involves an awareness of biblical teaching. This knowledge covers divinely revealed moral principles. It involves gearing one's life to moving in God's will, making progress in the direction of the goal which He sets before you. Paul aptly defined this: "I press on toward the goal to win the prize for which God has called me heavenward in Christ Jesus" (3:14).

Unfortunately, far too many believers in Christ become specialists in trivia. Have you ever met a person who is a specialist in sports trivia? He can tell you who led the American League in stolen bases in 1925; what pitcher held the record for consecutive walks in 1946; ad infinitum.

We should be aware that there is knowledge which is useless—and there is knowledge which is fruitful. As we study the Scriptures and allow the Holy Spirit to engraft into our lives the principles of God's Word, we become educated to a fuller understanding of God's love and grace. This knowledge frees us to move beyond theological trivia to a greater personal love for Jesus Christ.

A lay leader in my church shared how each morning he disciplines himself by reciting several key Scripture verses. In this way the positive input of God's Word bombards his thoughts. This process is influencing his spiritual growth to the glory of God.

The second quality is depth of insight. This is probably one of the least talked about but most important spiritual qualities we can have. Non-believers call this "common sense." From a spiritual perspective, it's the capacity to discriminate between right and wrong. Even more subtle is a person's capacity to distinguish between degrees of right. In most cases what is right and what is wrong can be quickly ascertained. It's much more difficult to know which of several legitimate courses of action is the most beneficial, or what loving response is most appropriate.

Solomon was blessed of God when he cried out for a discerning heart to govern God's people and for wisdom to distinguish between right and wrong. It pleased the Lord that Solomon had asked this (1 Kings 3:9-10).

The ability to discern is a special gift of God which is available to control and discipline our responses of love. It gives us perspective on how to relate to others. It helps protect us from that which is selfish and impure. It gives us the ability to apply right moral principles to special circumstances.

Life moves quickly and we can get caught up in its swift current similar to some logs which are pushed downstream. We can be just like one of those logs, unaware that a mile or two downstream there's a waterfall. All the logs are going in that direction. What seems right can be wrong. What seems loving can be unloving, if the action is undisciplined by the gift of discernment which the Lord wills for us to have. Part of the process of sanctification, or becoming mature persons, is that sensitizing by the Holy Spirit, which promotes the gift of discernment.

What Does Love Produce?

Love produces three basic by-products, each of which emerges from God's continuing sanctifying process in our lives. Paul states them in this way: "And this is my prayer: that your love may abound more and more in knowledge and depth of insight, so that you may be able to discern what is best and may be pure and blameless until the day of Christ, filled with the fruit of righteousness that comes through Jesus Christ—to the glory and praise of God" (Phil. 1:9).

One of love's by-products is correct moral choices. God wants us to be believers whose moral reflexes are developed, and Christians who approve what is excellent. He wants us to be prepared for Christ's coming, living lives which are sensitized to what is right. As we grow more and more in His love, increasing in knowledge and discernment, our moral reflexes become increasingly alert.

One morning, I was privileged to preach at a chapel service of the Baltimore Colts before the season's opening game with the Pittsburgh Steelers. The Colts' coach was in the second season of coaching this young team. He was trying to condition the athletes' reflexes into a winning pattern. He described to me the exciting challenge of helping young men develop professional efficiency. It takes time to develop a winning attitude. It takes time to mature.

This by-product of making correct moral choices is not a legalistic lifestyle. We're not trying to produce "Eagle Scout Christians" who win merit badges as they complete a list of requirements. That is a sterile, moralistic approach to Christian living. We don't try to live the Christian life by a set of laws or a list of do's and don'ts. If we see Christianity as a list of legal standards, we miss the joy of Christian living. A by-product of a growing love is a reflex system in which the Holy Spirit helps us approve what is truly excellent.

A second by-product of this lifestyle is the development of a high character. Paul's prayer is that his believer friends may be "pure and blameless until the day of Christ" (v. 10). This style of Christian living involves the desire to have victory over sin. Even though we'll slip and stumble, the forward-moving thrust is that of preparing us to appear before Jesus Christ at the day of judgment. Our blamelessness on that day will not be based on a perfect lifestyle achieved here; it will be the result of God's atoning work on our behalf. Our perfection is in Christ. A building of spiritual character through the years should show a steady growth pattern. As the years go by, we are better able to handle temptation because we have increased in our sensitivity to God and His Word. Our sincerity of lifestyle is one in which we look beyond our own interests. Our consciences are being sensitized to live for His will.

A third by-product is that our lives will produce good works. God wants us to be "filled with the fruit of righteousness that comes through Jesus Christ—to the glory and praise of God" (v. 11). As Paul said, "He who began a good work in you will carry it on to completion" (v. 6). Now he proclaims that Christ's work in us will evidence itself in our good works. James clearly argues this point: "What good is it, my brothers, if a man claims to have faith but has no deeds? Can such faith save him? . . . Show me your faith without deeds, and I will show you my faith by what I do. . . . You see that a person is justified by what he does and not by faith alone (James 2:14, 18, 24).

We must be aware that these good works are the products of our relationship with Jesus Christ. They are the outworking of His love in our lives. Fruitful living is an offshoot of our trust in Christ. A good conscience produces good works. Jesus referred to a branch being grafted into a tree. Later that branch bore fruit because of the life-sustaining quality coming through the trunk of that tree. Without that connection, the branch could not bear fruit. Without Christ, we cannot produce authentic Christian fruit (Matt. 7:16-20). Good fruit is a by-product of what He is doing in our lives.

We need to be very careful that we don't allow the fruit of His Spirit to become status symbols. The minute we begin to take pride in what we are doing for Christ, we negate the exciting potential of His action in our lives. This is the terrifying vulnerability we have as believers in Christ. An increased capacity for correct moral choices, the higher character which should mark the lives of believers, the fruitfulness of good works, can all turn to sterile spiritual rigidity, denying what God wants to do to the glory of Christ. Paul wrote to his believer friends, praying that they would increase more and more in love with knowledge and depth of insight. This would produce the necessary by-products in their lives, making them complete persons. We too can experience this exciting, maturing process.

2
How to Look at Reverses

Now I want you to know, brothers, that what has happened to me has really served to advance the Gospel. As a result, it has become clear throughout the whole palace guard and to everyone else that I am in chains for Christ. Because of my chains, most of the brothers in the Lord have been encouraged to speak the Word of God more courageously and fearlessly.

It is true that some preach Christ out of envy and rivalry, but others out of good will. The latter do so in love, knowing that I am put here for the defense of the Gospel. The former preach Christ out of selfish ambition, not sincerely, supposing that they can stir up trouble for me while I am in chains. But what does it matter? The important thing is that in every way, whether from false motives or true, Christ is preached. And because of this I rejoice.

Yes, and I will continue to rejoice, for I know that through your prayers and the help given by the Spirit of Jesus Christ, what has happened to me will turn out for my deliverance. I eagerly expect and hope that I will in no way be ashamed, but will have sufficient courage so that now as always Christ will be exalted in my body, whether by life or by death. For to me, to live is Christ and to die is gain (Phil. 1:12-21).

Yvonne and Raymond, both 22, met at a pub in Stafford, England to discuss divorce arrangements. Then Raymond drove Yvonne to his mother's house on his motorcycle. On the way, they crashed and were taken to a hospital. When the nurses heard about the impending divorce, they put the couple in adjoining beds. They were determined to patch up the marriage as well as the patients. "It worked," beamed Yvonne.

What seems to be bad can be good. Who would believe that a motorcycle accident could save a marriage? Sometimes the toughest experiences produce the best results. This isn't a popular message if you are looking for Christ as an escape from life's problems. It is a revolutionary insight into Christian living, if you are willing to make it your own. Take a look at Paul's experience and apply some basic lessons to your life.

The Way of the Cross

Don't be surprised when you run into difficulty. It's easy to be a Christian if you see Christ ushering you into a life of ease. Some of the promises in the Bible seem to suggest this. But coupled with those positive promises of God is the startling realization that the Christian life is not easy. This life involves the Cross. It's one of the toughest lifestyles you can choose.

Paul was writing from prison in Rome. Periodically, he reminded his Christian friends of the sufferings he had experienced. In the letter to the church at Corinth, he validated the genuineness of his commitment to Christ by listing the difficulties he had faced. He talked about greater labors and more imprisonments, with countless beatings leaving him near death:

Five times I received from the Jews the 40 lashes minus 1. Three times I was beaten with rods, once I was stoned, three times I was shipwrecked; I spent a night and a day in the open sea, I have been constantly on the move. I have been in danger from rivers, in danger from bandits, in danger from my own countrymen, in danger from Gentiles; in danger in the city, in danger in the country, in danger at sea; and in danger from false brothers. I have labored and toiled and have often gone without sleep; I have known hunger and thirst and have often gone

without food; I have been cold and naked. Besides
everything else, I face daily the pressure of my concern for
all the churches. Who is weak, and I do not feel weak?
Who is led into sin, and I do not inwardly burn? (2 Cor.
11:24-29)

Christian living is not an escape from trouble. Christ promised us
that we would have trouble in this world. Suffering is a basic
component of Christian experience.

When Paul described these sufferings, he was not talking about the
results of his sins. That was a different type of suffering. Today, if we
face problems as a result of our rebellion against God, we are not
suffering for the sake of Christ. Nor are we talking about suffering for
stupid mistakes. You and I have made our share! Paul's experience
was specific suffering because of his commitment to Jesus Christ. He
could have slid out from under this kind of suffering, and we can too.

A teenager described some of the temptations and pressures she
had faced when her friends urged her to join them in experimenting
with alcohol and drugs.

It's not easy to be a Christian teenager, one who is willing to swim
against the stream of popular peer pressure and suffer for the sake of
Christ. This kind of suffering leaves the teenager exposed to sneering,
jeering, and scorn, which wouldn't be there if he adapted or
compromised his Christian testimony.

Another example of suffering for Christ could be when your family
budget begins to feel the pinch of your sacrificial giving to His work.
After all, you could be spending your tithe on yourself to get relief
from the economic strain.

If at some point you face unpleasantness because of serving Christ,
thank God instead of copping out. You should thank Him for the
privilege of paying that small price which comes to the willing
disciple. Do you resent the cost of your discipleship? Are you
surprised when you feel the pinch? The pattern of the early church
was to rejoice in difficulties. In the latter part of the fifth chapter of
Acts, Luke describes the apostles taking a beating for their faith, and
then being charged not to speak in the name of Jesus: "The apostles
left the Sanhedrin, rejoicing because they had been counted worthy of

suffering disgrace for the Name. Day after day, in the temple courts and from house to house, they never stopped teaching and proclaiming the Good News that Jesus is the Christ" (Acts 5:41-42).

There is another example of one who counted the cost: "Moses ... refused to be known as the son of Pharaoh's daughter. He chose to be mistreated along with the people of God rather than to enjoy the pleasures of sin for a short time. He regarded disgrace for the sake of Christ as of greater value than the treasures of Egypt, because he was looking ahead to his reward" (Heb. 11:24-26).

Peter wrote, "But how is it to your credit if you receive a beating for doing wrong and endure it? But if you suffer for doing good and you endure it, this is commendable before God" (1 Peter 2:20).

It's easy to live the Christian life until you confront the Cross. Charles G. Finney wrote:

> There are many professors who are willing to do almost anything in religion that does not require self-denial. But when they are required to do anything that requires them to deny themselves—oh, that is too much! They think they are doing a great deal for God, and doing about as much as He ought in reason to ask, if they are only doing what they can do just as well as not; but they are not willing to deny themselves any comfort or convenience whatever for the sake of serving the Lord.
>
> They will not willingly suffer reproach for the name of Christ. Nor will they deny themselves the luxuries of life, to save the world from hell. So far are they from remembering that self-denial is a condition of discipleship that they do not know what self-denial is. (This quoted material was taken from a reprint which appeared in *The Presbyterian Journal,* Sept. 18, 1974, p. 13.)

The Gospel Advanced

Instead of complaining about his circumstances of imprisonment, Paul shared these words with his brothers and sisters in Philippi: "What has happened to me has really served to advance the Gospel. As a result, it has become clear throughout the whole palace guard and to everyone else that I am in chains for Christ. Because of my chains, most of the brothers in the Lord have been encouraged to speak the Word of God more courageously and fearlessly" (Phil. 1:12-14).

Paul could have complained about the heavy weight of the Cross. Instead, he expressed joy at what he had seen accomplished as a result of his difficult circumstances. Instead of his imprisonment destroying his ministry, the exact opposite had happened. Positives had been produced. The grim realities had worked to spread the Gospel. Why?

First, suffering for Christ stimulates public interest. Chained to a guard, Paul must have led a miserable life. Yet what an exciting opportunity for an evangelist. Hour upon hour, he had a captive audience. Then, when the guard shift changed, Paul had a new person with whom to share the meaning of a relationship with Jesus Christ. The Roman guards were so interested in the Gospel that they spread the good word. There is a great power in the witness of a consistent Christian life! Henrietta Mears states it so succinctly, "Your obstacles may become your pulpit."

Second, suffering for Christ authenticates one's witness. We talk about credibility. We become cynical about a politician who pretends to take courageous stands on popular issues. We want to see what stand he will take when that issue is no longer popular. Is he a phony? Or is he real? There's something refreshing about a person who is willing to pay the price of his convictions. How easy it would have been for Paul to slide out from under his imprisonment, saying simply, "I've pushed this issue too far. It would be better for me if I didn't appeal my case to Rome. I'll soft-pedal my convictions for a while and slip off into the community where I can reach people and preach with greater freedom." However, since Paul was unwilling to compromise, he authenticated the validity of his commitment to Jesus Christ.

You and I can show how seriously we take our commitment to Christ when the going gets tough. Difficulties resulting from what we believe help bring us to a deeper understanding of our need to depend on the Lord. When we pay the price of our convictions we become much more complete persons.

What is more repulsive than a moral chameleon? I have a friend who is a congenial "yes man." He adapts himself to whatever circumstances that he finds himself in. The world doesn't take his kind of Christianity seriously. The Scriptures do not urge us to be spiritual masochists, taking joy in self-inflicted pain. Rather, people respect us when they see us willing to pay the price of our commitment to Jesus Christ. As Paul says, "It has become known throughout the whole palace guard and to everyone else that I am in chains for Christ" (v. 13).

Third, suffering for Christ will stimulate other believers to new zeal. This is what happened at Rome. Paul wrote, "Most of the brothers in the Lord have been encouraged to speak the Word of God more courageously and fearlessly" (v. 14).

The date: July 1960. The place: Moscow, Russia. The setting: the obscure First Baptist Church, packed to overflowing on a Tuesday evening. It took me several days to find out where the congregation met. The taxi driver didn't want to let me off in front of the church with a plain facade. Never will I be the same after worshiping with those believers who paid a price for their witness. It had cost many of them jobs, position, and even family relationships to publicly express their faith in Christ. Etched on my memory forever is the glow of determined faithfulness to Christ which radiated from those believers in spite of their suffering.

The Love of Christ Is Contagious

Enthusiasm is contagious. Some advertisers cynically latch onto this principle, developing a phony lifestyle of enthusiasm to sell products.

On one occasion my former associate, Jim Stout, and I were in Washington, D.C. We went to an office to pick up some tickets for a concert. A volunteer secretary met us, exuding a vivacious, positive attitude. Finally, I commented on her enthusiastic approach to life. She admitted she had just completed a course in PMA—Positive Mental Attitude.

This is not the contagious enthusiasm which marked the life of Paul. He had a steadfast, purposeful commitment which was born out of joys and sorrows, good times and bad. That steadiness of commitment was the contagious element. He was concerned that Jesus Christ be preached.

Instead of sitting in a corner of a prison cell, weeping over circumstances, he sang hymns of praise to God. This conviction had impressed his jailers at Philippi 10 years before. And now in Rome this same steady commitment was continuing to bear fruit. Such all-absorbing interest bends all circumstances to its service. That's why Paul could say, "I know what it is to be in need, and I know what it is to have plenty. I have learned the secret of being content in any and every situation, whether well-fed or hungry, whether living in plenty or want" (Phil. 4:12). He had the assurance that he could do all things through Christ who strengthened him. Everything filtered through this purpose.

Billy Graham once told me when I was a very young pastor, "As long as you are willing to burn yourself out for Jesus Christ, the world will come if for no other reason than to watch the flame."

The problem is that so many of us Christians are more like ice water than fire. We have been so coddled by our society and so privileged by our circumstances, that our lack of suffering has made us impotent in our service to the Lord.

We've allowed ourselves to become ingrown, protective of our own territory. No arguments can become harsher than those over theological subtleties. No jealousies can go deeper than those directed to one who seems to have the blessing of the Lord on his life.

Paul expressed such enthusiasm to communicate the Gospel that he was willing to put aside petty rivalries. He talked about an inclusive love of Jesus Christ, which called all who had pledged themselves to the risen Christ, brothers.

To Live Is Christ . . . or Career . . . or Family . . . or Ideas

Excitement flashed from the energetic young stockbroker's eyes as he described his moneymaking plan. He had offered his financial consulting skills to neighbors. Response had been tremendous. He told me, "My career is the most important thing in my life!"

Frank and Mary bought a cottage in the woods. They had saved for it a long time. "We're going there every weekend," said Frank. "It's our greatest joy."

Frank's motive seems quite admirable. His family is important. In a time when many families are breaking up, his attitude would be commended by many.

Peter, in his late 50s, had taught philosophy for many years. He loved ideas. Brilliant, sophisticated, he lived in his book-lined study. His theme could easily be, "For me to live is knowledge."

Each of these had set his course and had made primary commitments to his lifestyle. Each was a good example of one who knew where he was headed in life.

What Is Your Center of Living?

Stop for a moment. Ask yourself, "Why do I live? What is the ultimate drive in my life?" The answer is, "For me to live is _____." (You fill in the blank.)

There is an alternate lifestyle for you as a Christian. Paul stated it succinctly: "For to me, to live is Christ" (Phil. 1:21). This declaration sets you free from the world's standards. This affirmation gives a point of reference by which you can judge all you do, say, and are. Christ makes it possible for you to really live.

First, Christ is the Source of life. He said, "I have come that they may have life, and have it to the full" (John 10:10). Paul described his own relationship with Christ: "I have been crucified with Christ and I no longer live, but Christ lives in me. The life I live in the body, I live by faith in the Son of God who loved me and gave Himself for me" (Gal. 2:20).

God wants us to open our lives to Him. He wants us to accept Him as Lord. Jesus Christ wants to be our God. He wants us to live for Him, so we can find what real living is all about.

Second, Christ is our Model for living. Management consultant Peter Drucker emphasizes how important it is to have the right model of leadership in business. Right models are necessary for all of life. Jesus Christ is the very highest Model for living.

One of the most beautiful books ever written is entitled *The Imitation of Christ* by Thomas á Kempis. He refers often to following

Christ's example. What a model to follow! He was the One who really knew how to live with an expendable lifestyle. He enjoyed pleasure, while at the same time, He knew how to say no. He had fame, but it didn't go to His head. He could move comfortably with both the rich and the poor. He had all power at His disposal, yet He refused to exploit it for egotistical purposes. In Christ we see a true model.

Third, Christ is the Sustainer of your life. He is the power supply which never runs out. Through His Spirit you are energized for quality living. However, you'll only be able to realize His sustaining and energizing influence if you stay plugged in. You can unplug—by your attitudes, by your rebellious lifestyles, by a willful, selfish nature. It's too easy to pull away from that constantly available flow of energy which the Lord wants to supply.

Jesus promises to carry you through this life if you let Him. The way will not always be easy. You will have your ups and downs. There will be those times when you will wonder if He is capable of following through on His promises.

At the same time, as a Christian who is living for Christ, you know how to live life at its best. You learn what is important and what isn't. With the Lord's help, you learn more fully how to coordinate the social, intellectual, physical, and spiritual dimensions of your existence.

You'll find that this one unifying principle will bring about creative living which is a dynamic contrast to the hedonistic approach of many today, who bounce from one superficial stimulus to another. The Christian is alive because he is growing, maturing, developing his God-given resources. How different from the philosophy expressed by people such as those who appear on the Johnny Carson show. Night after night Mr. Carson conducts an entertaining crusade in the living rooms, dens, and bedrooms of American homes. He preaches the philosophy of hedonism, urging you by his subtle comments and those of his guests to do what feels good for the moment.

If you want some help in finding out what your center of living is, try this: Sit down and write your own obituary. Try to figure out what one honest key sentence could be uttered at your funeral to capsulize your life.

"He surely made it big in business." Or, "He never let his business success take his eyes off Christ and the needs of his fellowman." Or, "He certainly made a failure of his life." Or, "In spite of business setbacks, he claimed the Lord's strength." Or, "She went around complaining all the time." Or, "Although for 10 years she fought a losing battle with cancer, she communicated a radiance of life and was a source of strength to her family."

Does Our Center of Living Prepare Us to Die?

That's a point-blank frontal question! Death is coming our way, no matter what precautions we take against it.

It's fascinating to see the change which has come over American society. The previous generation was afraid to talk about both death and sex. The present generation is afraid to talk about death! In our perpetual quest for the fountain of youth, we have applied a cosmetic surface to our existence which tries to cover the reality of our inevitable departure from this world.

Death involves mystery, but for those who don't have their lives centered on Jesus, death involves speculation, uncertainty, fear. To die is life's most desperate venture. There's always the possibility of becoming a nonentity.

Then there's the possibility of life after death. The Bible is true; there is a hell. Failure to talk about it doesn't remove its existence. To deny the fact of hell doesn't make hell any less a fact. The Bible reveals facts about eternity. We are immortal persons. Someday we will step into eternity. We'll either spend it in the presence of Jesus Christ in an exhilarating, productive lifestyle or we'll spend it in isolation from Him and all that is of utmost quality.

Paul wrote, "For to me, to live is Christ and to die is gain" (Phil. 1:21). Christ frees us to live or die. Through Him we can have a quality of perspective which can release us from uptightness over life and death. We can be provided with a whole new perspective on both living and dying. We can have the promises of Christ who gives the assurance that He has gone to prepare a place for us. Assurance that we will spend eternity in heaven with Him releases us to a much freer lifestyle here on earth.

Paul talked about being hard-pressed between the two—wanting one moment to live—the next moment to die. He said, "I am torn between the two: I desire to depart and be with Christ, which is better by far; but it is more necessary for you that I remain in the body" (vv. 23-24).

This is not a melancholy, suicidal death wish. This is the buoyant statement of one who knows that Christ has covered all the bases, both in this life and the life beyond. It's an expansion of God's provision for the future which holds us steady in the present. When we spend eternity in the heavens with Jesus Christ, we will be free from pain, agony, hurts, and broken relationships.

What Christian at some moments has not thought how wonderful it would be to leave this planet to be forever in the presence of Christ? But combined with recurring joyous thoughts is an immediate snapback similar to that of Paul. We can feel the tug to be with Christ. Yet His very provision for our death gives us a greater compulsion to live, free to serve Him, and to follow His great commission. Christianity in its finest sense does not produce indifference to life, but more concern to help others. Christ frees us to be ourselves, since we are not tied to false centers of life. In Him, we are free to live or to die!

I heard Festo Kivengere, an Anglican bishop from Uganda, Africa, tell the following story: During severe persecution in Burundi, an African believer was confronted by a pistol in his face. This Christian said to his would-be killer, "Before you shoot, please let me express three things. First, I love you because Jesus Christ loves you. Second, I love my country. Third, let me sing you this song." Then radiantly that believer began singing:

Out of my bondage, sorrow and night,
Jesus, I come, Jesus, I come.
Into Thy freedom, gladness and light,
Jesus, I come to Thee.
Out of my sickness into Thy health,
Out of my want and into Thy wealth,
Out of my sin and into Thyself,
Jesus, I come to Thee.

That's real freedom! No, his life was not spared. That was no clever gimmick. He was free to live or to die.

There are basically two theories of life. One can be tersely stated, "For me to live is self, and to die is loss and uncertainty." The other is, "For me to live is Christ, and to die is gain." We choose which way we will go!

3
Maintaining a
High Reputation

Whatever happens, conduct yourselves in a manner worthy of the Gospel of Christ. Then, whether I come and see you or only hear about you in my absence, I will know that you stand firm in one spirit, contending as one man for the faith of the Gospel without being frightened in any way by those who oppose you. This is a sign to them that they will be destroyed, but that you will be saved—and that by God. For it has been granted to you on behalf of Christ not only to believe on Him, but also to suffer for Him, since you are going through the same struggle you saw I had, and now hear that I still have (Phil. 1:27-30).

In some Christian circles, the concept of developing a special reputation has been frowned on as a desire to be well thought of by people of the world. To gain acceptance in the world's crowd, to have everyone thinking well of you, to have a reputable personality is worldly. Or these people have been placed in the pharisaical category because "they loved praise from men more than praise from God" (John 12:43).

Unfortunately, because of strong preaching on negatives for several decades, many of our evangelical churches have gained a "We don't do this, we don't do that" reputation. Some follow a rather narrowly defined list of don'ts which have become well known by outsiders. Such a reputation we no longer need. We need the reputation of being "doers of the Word" (James 1:22, KJV). That's the reputation which harmonizes with Paul's instructions to the Philippians.

The Apostle John described the reputation of the church at Sardis in some extremely uncomplimentary terms: "I know your deeds; you have a reputation of being alive, but you are dead." Then the Lord exclaimed, "Wake up!" (Rev. 3:1-2)

Paul's loving instructions to the Christians at Philippi were that they develop a reputation "worthy of the Gospel of Christ." This was to be done through their manner of conduct. He said they should do this whether or not he was able to come to Philippi to check up on them.

A Reputation Worthy of the Gospel

What were the main elements of this reputation? Paul contended their main reputation would focus on how they reacted to conflict with each other and the witness they presented to others.

Paul used the words of battle. He talked of "contending." He referred to "those who oppose you" and about "standing firm." He talked about being engaged in conflict. He added such strong words as "destruction" and "salvation." Each of these references was packed briefly into four verses (Phil. 1:27-30).

Throughout the New Testament, other references were made to spiritual conflict. In writing to the Romans, Paul described an internal spiritual warfare between sin and righteousness: "But I see another law at work in the members of my body, waging war against the law of my mind and making me a prisoner of the law of sin at work within my members" (Rom. 7:23).

Then he described the power of God which works in believers to pull down the strongholds of sin. "The weapons we fight with are not the weapons of the world. On the contrary, they have divine power to demolish strongholds" (2 Cor. 10:4).

Paul also alerted us to the invisible foe. "For our struggle is not against flesh and blood, but against the rulers, against the authorities, against the power of this dark world and against the spiritual forces of evil in the heavenly realms. Therefore put on the full armor of God, so that when the day of evil comes, you may be able to stand your ground" (Eph. 6:12-13).

Paul encouraged young Timothy to engage in a good warfare. Later on he enlisted Timothy to "fight the good fight, holding on to faith" (1 Tim. 1:18-19). In his next letter he warned Timothy that a soldier must not get bogged down with civilian pursuits. A good solider of Christ sticks in the battle.

Are You Ready for Conflict?

But you say, "I came to Jesus to find peace, not conflict. I wanted to be free from conflict, especially within myself. I have no desire to deliberately get involved in conflict. There's no enjoyment in that!"

No, conflict is fun only in games. But true Christian living is not a mock battle. We're not just playing war games. Our head-on encounter with the world does produce conflict.

But conflict is not *all* bad. It can actually be good for us. In preparation for my first doctoral exam, I read a couple of books about conflict. In the sociological study called "conflict management," I discovered that though conflict can be bad, sophisticated analysts see conflict as essential to creative living. Speed B. Leas and Paul Kittlaus define conflict as the striking together of two objects trying to occupy the same space at the same time. They go on to note that conflicting goals are two purposes or objectives that cannot occupy the same place at the same time (*Time Management*, Abingdon). Ross Stagner says conflict is "a situation in which two or more human beings desire goals which they perceive as being attainable by one or the other but not by both" (*Psychology of Personality*, McGraw).

Though conflict can be bad, these sociology specialists are quick to point out that it can also be good.

What Is Good about Conflict?

First, conflict energizes us. It influences many of our bodily functions, especially in stimulating the activity of the adrenal glands. Suddenly, when confronted by a serious threat, our mental and physical capacities are stretched out of status quo lethargy. The threat goads us into action.

Some writers and preachers function best only under pressure. Give them a year to leisurely work and they can't produce one good sermon or chapter. Put them under weekly pressure and they perform superbly. There's nothing like a deadline to stimulate the mind into productive activity.

Second, conflict helps establish our identity. If we could live in a world free from tension it would be easy to become lost in the crowd—to make no waves. But if we must confront a difficulty, we immediately identify ourselves. When we face a temptation, the battle lines are drawn as to whether or not we identify with being persons of God or with those who play it safe. Jesus used conflict as a means to establish the identity of men and women. He said, "He who is not with Me is against Me, and he who does not gather with Me scatters" (Matt. 12:30).

Third, conflict unifies the body of Christ. Put a church into difficult times and you'll find an *esprit de corps* which binds Christians firmly together to accomplish common purposes. Granted, this positive use of conflict can be exploited, especially if a leader becomes dictatorial. But most often conflict leads toward good results.

In the political realm, conflict often unites people. Israel is the best example of that. Syrian military regimes in overwhelming numbers have, on occasion, invaded Israel. In each case Israel seemed to have absolutely no chance of winning. But internal foes joined each other as they took on external foes. Israel won again and again.

So conflict can actually serve good purposes. It's not all bad. And the avoidance of conflict in our Christian lives is ultimately costly. Surely there are ways in which we can avoid spiritual warfare, but we do it at the price of our own soul's development. My prayer is that we don't try to escape the spiritual warfare which is part of every dedicated Christian's life.

Satan is alive and well. In fact, he is on the attack daily. He would like to decimate our spiritual lives. He would like to cut the church of Jesus Christ into infinitesimal pieces. His attack is subtle. It's not always a clearly defined battle in which men with black hats confront those of us who pride ourselves on wearing white hats.

You and I are familiar with some of Satan's more obvious temptations. We have sensed his attacks as he paints appealing pictures of fleshly sins. Yet as we grow in our spiritual sensitivity, we discern some more delicate lines between right and wrong. We know what we should do. We are painfully aware when we fail. Using sophisticated methods, Satan prefers to attack those of us who are more spiritually mature. In this way he can cause us to doubt and sometimes question the very existence of the Lord we claim to love and serve.

Often vague allusions to the power and deadliness of satanic attacks on the spirit of dedicated Christians are made. But Amy Carmichael, who spent 55 years as a missionary to China, cuts through this pious and vague language in her book *God's Missionary* (Christian Literature Crusade). She outlines six of Satan's most subtle attacks on believers and notes that these are particularly troublesome to missionaries. Let's go over each of these, seeing how they tie into our experience as contemporary believers.

Satan's Attacks

Attack #1: discouragement. Miss Carmichael describes the penetrating, hissing whisper of Satan in the ear of a self-sacrificing missionary, saying, "How much more you might have done for God at home!" And then, the missionary begins to think, *Those years of language study before the vital roots of ministry begin to grow—that solitude in an idolatrous city, faced with a pagan culture.* The black sea of discouragement sweeps in wave upon wave. His very foundations begin to quiver under the impact of the tremendous floods. And discouragement hits at the moment he's seemingly made the greatest sacrifice for the Lord.

Attack #2: the subtle seepage of nominal Christianity. When we first come to Christ, there is a buoyant enthusiasm which enables us to burst into situations of witnessing where angels fear to tread. We feel our love for Christ so keenly. We speak enthusiastically and sincerely. But gradually the sharp edges of our Christian testimonies wear smooth. It's hard to maintain a cutting edge of glowing faith when we are surrounded by nominal, lackadaisical Christians. This is harder than being thrust into a hostile environment. Our vital prayer needs to be "from slack contentment keep us free." Part of our spiritual conflict is to confront head-on the tendency toward lackluster Christianity. It's part of Satan's clever attack. I know. My wife Anne and I have experienced this tendency to live and let live. It's easy to cleverly rationalize that we shouldn't force our faith on anyone else. In the process we find ourselves diluting the potency of witnessing for Christ.

Attack #3: spiritual flattery. Oh, how much fun it is to be admired. Isn't it great to be put on a spiritual pedestal? It's addictive—the praise of well-meaning, wonderful people. Because it's a natural part of human nature to want to be appreciated, it's easy to crave the praise of fellow Christians. We thrive on compliments. When they no longer come, it's also easy to begin questioning the suitability of our Christian calling. Or we settle back, comfortable in the accomplishments of the past. We kid ourselves into thinking we have arrived.

Attack #4: discontentment. This is different from discouragement. Not only do we become discouraged, we also become boxed in with unhappiness. Bored with life, we develop an aversion to the place where God has put us. People begin to get on our nerves—the same people who were once our spiritual confidants.

We face this struggle. Judgmentalism begins to creep into our lifestyle. It starts out innocently, even as we dedicate ourselves to vital Christian values. Then this attitude twists and wiggles its way into a rigidity of temperament which condemns others. Never do we judge our own spiritual inconsistencies. Putting ourselves on a spiritual level above others, we become discontented.

Attack #5: dryness. Ever felt spiritually arid? We cry out in prayer, only to find our throats parched to the point that no sounds seem to go up to the Lord. It's in times like these that we need spiritual refreshment. Some of the finest devotional material has been written by those who have gone through times of spiritual dryness. That's what prompted Mrs. Charles Cowman to write her classic *Streams in the Desert* (Zondervan).

Attack #6: depression. Ever come to a point of just plain, downright gloom for apparently no reason at all? Satan has the capacity to get us into this mental state. It's not our fault. We're not to blame. If Satan can put us into that mood, he knows that we're all the more vulnerable to his attacks. Some depression needs delicate psychiatric or psychological help. However, much of it is a melancholy state of mind induced by spiritually off-base movements.

How Do We Beat Off Satan's Subtle Attacks?

We can run up the white flag and surrender. There are plenty of good reasons to check out of vital Christian living. It is a costly life. It has its highly complicated aspects. We can write it off as an unrealistic lifestyle.

Or we can find scapegoats. We can blame every weakness and defeat on someone else, or on something else. I noticed this tendency during Richard Nixon's last days as President. Without question, he made some serious mistakes for which he is accountable. At the same time, we Americans immediately had a convenient whipping boy, a "scapegoat" onto which we could pin the blame for everything that would go wrong during the next decade or two. How unfortunate, this scapegoating tendency.

We do the same thing spiritually. We blame our partners, our parents, our churches for everything which goes wrong, avoiding certain spiritual realities. We blame everyone but ourselves!

Instead of running up the white flag, or finding someone else on whom to blame the difficult circumstances of our spiritual lives, we can willingly throw ourselves into the battle of Christian conflict. Instead of resenting God for allowing us to come into difficult times, we can allow His Spirit to work a purging process on the inner person, making us more usable in His service.

Three words capsulize Paul's description of your Christian battle:

First, you are called to "steadfastness." He writes, "Stand firm in one spirit" (Phil. 1:27). There is no room for retreat. How emphatic were the words of Martin Luther as he told his accusers, "Here I stand." He was encouraged by the Lord and became determined to hold his ground. A choir director shared this sage advice, comparing an individual's life to that of a postage stamp: "Think of the postage stamp—its ability to stick to one thing until its job is done!" Steadfastness is a key to the Christian battle.

Second, "unity" is essential. If you are to survive in Christian conflict, you have to find the release of being broadened past your isolationism and individualism. Paul vividly calls you to stand firm in one spirit, "contending as one man for the faith of the Gospel" (v. 27).

You simply can't go it alone in the Christian life. This is a corporate affair. You and I must be "one in the spirit, one in the Lord." You and I need to have "one mind." Imagine a soldier going out to fight a battle armed only with a BB gun. What chance does he have? He needs the proper equipment. He also needs colleagues in battle. The description Paul gives is of a band of swordsmen working together. "Like a mighty army moves the church of God."

All too often you and I strike off in isolated forays. Then we wonder why we lose. Why are we so vulnerable? Because we've neglected our responsibility to unify in the common service of Jesus Christ. This is why He established the church. And today, as never before, there's a need for believers, regardless of denomination, to unify in Jesus Christ to battle the forces opposed to the Gospel.

Third, you are "unconquerable" in battle. You need not be frightened by your opponents, because the outcome of the battle is certain. Paul writes that you aren't to be "frightened in any way by those who oppose you. This is a sign to them that they will be destroyed, but that you will be saved—and that by God" (v. 28). The outcome is already determined. You shouldn't turn aside. You are on the winning side. Paul wrote this from prison. He had confidence. He was quick to say, "I've been through this myself. I've suffered. But I know that all is well."

Christ Is Victor

This is the privilege of suffering for the sake of Christ. Yet this suffering really lasts only for a moment. It's like watching a World War II movie. We can identify with the pain and the anxiety, as we see that desperate war come to life on the screen. Our hearts are broken as we see the gaunt, desperately emaciated figures of some of those six million Jews clamoring at the barbed wire fences, being herded into extermination. Ethiopia is invaded. France falls. London is bombed. Submarines threaten the United States.

But wait. It's just a movie. We know the results. The Allies win. Paul writes that Satan will be destroyed. Our salvation is sure. Christ is the Victor.

Paul's opening words were, "Whatever happens, conduct yourselves in a manner worthy of the Gospel of Christ" (v. 27). He's calling us to worthy living. He's talking about right deportment. The words *be worthy* literally mean "behave like good citizens." He's calling us to a civic consciousness because we are citizens of heaven. It's a costly citizenship. It was purchased by the death of Jesus Christ. It was sealed by His resurrection. He calls us to wear our citizenship openly, and willingly to engage in Christian conflict to serve the Lord. Always!

4
Servanthood

If you have any encouragement from being united with Christ,
if any comfort from His love, if any fellowship with the Spirit, if
any tenderness and compassion, then make my joy complete
by being like-minded, having the same love, being one in spirit
and purpose. Do nothing out of selfish ambition or vain
conceit, but in humility consider others better than yourselves.
Each of you should look not only to your own interests, but also
to the interests of others.
    Your attitude should be the same as that of Christ Jesus:
        Who, being in very nature God,
            did not consider equality with God
                something to be grasped,
        but made Himself nothing,
            taking the very nature of a servant,
            being made in human likeness.
    And being found in appearance as a man,
        He humbled Himself
        and became obedient to death—
            even death on a cross!
           (Phil. 2:1-8)

For at least the past 50 years, evangelical (or biblical, or Bible-
believing) Christians have been known for their attacks on church

unity. They've preached against it. They've been uncooperative at local levels and have denounced any getting together among believers.

We have only to attend Bible conferences or evangelistic meetings, open to believers of all denominations, to discover it isn't the denominational or local church name tag that counts. There's an immediate unity in Jesus Christ regardless of differences in interpretations of some doctrines such as baptism, church government, and the Second Coming of Christ. When Jesus Christ and the Word of God are central, believers have an immediate camaraderie with other believers.

Rather than tearing down that camaraderie, or sheepishly admitting church unity might be possible, we ought to look for those things about which Paul was concerned: "encouragement from being united with Christ . . . comfort from His love . . . fellowship with the Spirit . . . tenderness and compassion" (v. 1). Christ intimated we'll discover these by "being like-minded, having the same love, being one in spirit and purpose" (v. 2).

Though the Scriptures warn us against apostasy and false doctrine, we shouldn't continually spend time lambasting other Christians. If we do, there's serious reason to question our motives. We rarely build up Christians of other denominations and persuasions by attacking them. Believers are best fortified against apostasy and false doctrine by positive, well-studied-out explanations of biblical truths. Sometimes we attack others because we desire to enhance our own reputations as defenders of the faith. Paul warns against such selfish ambition. "Do nothing out of selfish ambition or vain conceit, but in humility consider others better than yourselves" (v. 3). Wow! This strikes a blow at all self-aggrandizing. It places servanthood on a high pedestal—even though the servant-type person never climbs onto a pedestal.

Servanthood Recognizes the Good in Others

Paul tells the Philippians, "Each of you should look not only to your own interests, but also to the interests of others" (v. 4). Those who make personal interests priority No. 1 usually care little about the interests of others. In fact, they readily trample others in order to fulfill their own desires. And this can happen to those in a Bible-believing church as well as in the world. Some people have a lust for power. They want to be out front. They want their opinions known and accepted. Or else! Often they trample over the views of fellow believers, and denounce well-known Christian leaders with whom they disagree. Paul's presentation of the attitude of Jesus Christ seems so contrary to the attitudes discussed above. He says, "Let this mind be in you, which was also in Christ Jesus" (Phil. 2:5, KJV)—the mind of a servant!

Yet in no way did the apostle squelch the concept of diversity. Paul stresses a diversity of spiritual gifts. (See 1 Cor. 14 and Rom. 12.) There's no sameness in abilities. God dresses His people in colorful array—not in drab uniforms, which brings glory to the person of Jesus Christ. So when Paul calls the church at Philippi—or Pittsburgh—or Portland—or Podunk—to unity, he is quite aware that churches are made up of a wide diversity of people. Three specific people at the church of Philippi differed greatly: Lydia, a wealthy seller of purple goods; a poor slave girl who had demons cast out; and the jailer who responded to the Good News of salvation after an earthquake. Could we ask for three more different people? Only the Lord knows how many other personality types complicated that church's membership rolls. Could they enjoy unity?

Discord is always possible wherever there are people. We couldn't ask for more potential disunity than in a metropolitan church today. Some drive from the suburbs; others walk from nearby apartments. Some may be 80 years old; others aren't quite 18. Their lot may be chairman of the board—or janitor. Some like Beethoven and Bach, while others prefer Hoagy or Ralph Carmichael. Some would still like to rent their pews, while others find that idea repulsive.

There should be unity in our diversity. Unity comes when we understand that unity is not uniformity. Unity comes when those of us with extremely diverse backgrounds rally around a common center. That center is our shared personal trust in Jesus Christ as Saviour and Lord. That unity is enhanced as we become servants one to another.

How to Produce Unity

Paul called the church at Philippi to unity, sketching five reasons to put aside party differences and move toward a oneness of common faith.

First, he appeals to the oneness of our experience in Jesus Christ as he writes, "If you have any encouragement from being united with Christ" (Phil. 2:1). When we share a common experience in which our lives have been changed by the power of Christ, we have an automatic oneness.

Second, he appeals to the power of Christian love. Different, yes. Yet love is present as Paul says, "If any comfort from His love" (v. 1).

Third, he appeals to our common fellowship in the Holy Spirit. All believers have the Holy Spirit in their lives. He writes, "If any fellowship with the Spirit" (v. 1).

Fourth, Paul appeals to the simple human emotions of pity and compassion.

Fifth, and finally, he appeals to his own need as he says, "Look, I'm in prison. You love me. I've worked hard for you. Make me happy by showing your unity in the midst of your diversity." He urges, "Make my joy complete."

Appealing to the common grounds which pull the body of Christ together, Paul describes what similar qualities we should have in the midst of diversity. They are two in number:

We are to be like-minded—because of what God has done for us in Christ. We are to agree on the basics. God has revealed Himself to us. We have His Word. There is a common ground of knowledge. In spite of all our differences, we are to be of similar mind. Our thoughts are fixed on the person of Jesus Christ. We are indebted to Him. We are related to Him. Therefore, we reflect the image of our Father in heaven.

Ever stopped to look at a child whose parents you know well? Isn't it uncanny how that child has the image of the parent stamped upon his features? Those deep-set eyes, that fairness of skin, the unmistakable pug nose. There's no mistaking who the mother is, or the father. Even husbands and wives seem to begin to resemble each other after years of living together. Likewise, those who have become children of

God through Jesus Christ take on more and more of the spiritual characteristics of the Saviour.

We are to be one in spirit and purpose. There's love where there's a commonness of purpose, a shared experience. Being a part of the family makes the difference. When my secretary's mother fell and broke her shoulder, there was no question what should be done. Several decades separated them. Their interests weren't the same. But they were family. In oneness of mind and love, Ruth ministered to her 80-year-old mother, opened her home and life, and gave of her time.

Two brothers play together, bouncing up and down on their bunk beds. They have their fights. But they are brothers. They are part of a family. Something about a blood tie, as different as they may become, holds them together.

Paul urges the church to be "of the same mind, having the same love, being one in spirit and purpose." That's the family of God at work!

What Destroys Unity?

There's something that can easily destroy unity. It's called *individualism*. There's a real danger in individualism in the Christian faith.

God has created us as individuals. He places a premium on our uniqueness. However, He doesn't value our uniqueness at the expense of our brothers or sisters in Christ. We cannot go it alone in the Christian faith. Nor should we allow others to stumble through life without our help.

It's so easy for our faith to be self-centered. The church at Philippi was a fine group of believers. Yet Paul felt it was his responsibility to remind them of their tendency toward self-centeredness. He wrote, "Do nothing out of selfish ambition or vain conceit" (v. 3). There was only one reason to give that kind of command. Apparently some believers were inclined toward selfishness and conceit. All of us have these tendencies. Some of us hide them better than others. Underneath the surface lurks this ugly two-headed monster.

Have you heard Reverend Ike on the radio? He tells the faithful how to become wealthy. If you write in today, he'll send you his success idea for each month.

But he's not the only one. The idea seems quite prevalent in evangelical Christianity. We all want to be successful. Therefore many schemes for becoming successful persons have been attached to the Christian faith. Paul questions the motive and the price of such success.

You and I wouldn't fall for the promises of Reverend Ike. Or would we? We apply self-help techniques to find precious peace of mind. We look for promises of quick healing.

I'm reminded of the following sad story: For months a teenager had been sick. She heard one television preacher say, "Trust the Lord and He will give you healing." She took him at his word. She agonized in daily prayer; still she remained sick. Now her mind was loaded with doubts about the reliability of God's promises.

Who's to blame? Is God? Not for a moment. It's a sincere but false premise of the preacher who promises something which even the Apostle Paul didn't achieve. Reflect on how Paul begged, agonizing in prayer on three different occasions, that God would remove his thorn in the flesh. Was it epilepsy? Was it some disease of the eyes? We don't know for certain. This supersaint didn't receive instant or even slow healing. He went through life with his thorn in the flesh and didn't turn his back on his Saviour. In fact, his life was all the richer through his suffering. In the process he did much more for others. Probably his infirmity enhanced his servanthood because it gave him a clearer understanding of the sufferings of fellow saints.

Our religion can quickly become self-centered. William Barclay suggests these three reasons as the biggest causes of discord among Christians: (1) selfish ambition; (2) the desire for personal prestige, which for some is greater than the temptation of wealth; (3) the concentration on self (*The Letters to the Philippians, Colossians, and Thessalonians,* Westminster Press, p. 47). These three combine to eliminate the importance of others. In the process, they cause disunity.

Antidotes to Selfishness

Paul suggests two antidotes for this selfishness:

Suggestion 1: Humbly consider others better than yourself. That's hard, isn't it? We work hard at being better than everybody else. We master the game of competition. We learn how to come out on top. But do we really end up on top? Henrietta Mears said it this way: "I am willing to be third." Are you? Am I? That's the essence of humility. That's the essence of servanthood. That's the attitude of Jesus Christ.

This doesn't mean we shouldn't do good jobs. It doesn't mean we shouldn't strive for excellence. It's a question of how we view ourselves.

Do we do our best to beat out someone else? Or do we do our best possible work in service to meet the needs of others? Are we willing to build up others even at our own expense? How many lessons do we have to learn when it comes to counting others better than ourselves? It doesn't come easy. And I have to preach this sermon most loudly to myself!

One of the great spirits of Christian servanthood is Dr. Christy Wilson, Jr. His example has taught me much. This self-effacing man of God would be embarrassed to know he had been praised in a book. He has a Christlike quality of encouraging others to be more than they are. Most of the last two decades of his life have been spent on the mission fields of Afghanistan. Today, he's on the faculty of Gordon-Conwell Theological Seminary. Even though his teaching is great, I am certain that many young people will find encouragement for future ministry through his humble and individual counsel.

Suggestion 2: Each of you should look not only to your own interests, but also to the interests of others. This doesn't put down our own importance. This only enhances how important we are. Our brothers, our sisters in Christ have interests just as important as ours. They need us. We need them. It's time to get out of ourselves.

Do you have a broken relationship with another person? Are you having trouble with discord, disharmony in the husband-wife, parent-child, fellow church member relationships? This week, why not make a list of five things you can do that you know that other person would love to have you do? Pray about each item. Get to work doing them. Then write down what the response was to each action. You'll be amazed at the positive reactions. Doing this in a genuine spirit of Christian love will get you out of your own interests.

Not long ago a local retail clerk came to my office. He shared details of problems he was having with his boss. He was depressed and frustrated with his job. In just a few moments we twisted the situation around so that he was no longer looking only at his own interests, but also at the interests of his boss. What problems did the boss have that made him act the way he did? This young man turned around and walked out of the church with a spring in his steps. He'd never thought of it that way. God had placed him in that business to have a ministry. Anticipating the interests of others produces harmony.

Called to Servanthood

What it all boils down to is that we are called to be servants. Ouch! Servants? Who wants to be a servant?

Let me ask a frank question. Would you like to be like Jesus Christ? Is there anyone in all human history whom you'd rather be? What would you really give to be like Christ? Paul combines all of the suggestions for Christian unity into the following description of Jesus. Capsuled in these verses is some of life's most explosive material—material which can revolutionize any Christian's life!

"Your attitude should be the same as that of Christ Jesus: who being in very nature God, did not consider equality with God something to be grasped, but made Himself nothing, taking the very nature of a servant, being made in human likeness. And being found in appearance as a man, He humbled himself" (Phil. 2:5-8).

What a description of Jesus! He was a servant. He gave Himself for others. Catch the rhythm? Here is one identical with God. God Himself who humbled Himself and became a man. He emptied Himself. He took the form of a servant. See the contrast between the humble Christ washing His disciples' feet and the power-oriented, success syndrome of Rome? Or the success syndrome so dominant in American culture? Jesus even went to the Cross. By losing Himself He exalted Himself. He rose triumphant in the ultimate service to others.

Jesus didn't reserve this exciting principle for Himself. He taught it to others. He said, "If anyone wants to be first, he must be the very last, and the servant of all" (Mark 9:35). He emphasized that the master will end up being the servant and the one who truly serves will hold the scepter. Jesus wasn't teaching gimmicks. This wasn't a clever sales course. It was a liberating course for life with purpose.

This lifestyle of servanthood involves a radical restructuring of our value systems. We're so used to seeing success as quantity and not quality. It's easy to get caught up in the numbers game, and frankly I don't like to wash smelly feet!

Once again, we as Christians are to transform the world by acting on the principles Christ taught us. Peter Drucker may not fully realize the implications of what he's saying when he talks about upward and downward authority in his book *The Effective Executive.* He writes, "The man who focuses on efforts and who stresses his downward authority is a subordinate no matter how exalted his title and rank. But the man who focuses on contribution and who takes responsibility for results, no matter how junior, is in the most literal sense of the phrase, 'top management'" (Harper and Row, p. 53). This is a management application of a spiritual principle.

Dr. Clarence Macartney, for many years minister of the First Presbyterian Church in Pittsburgh, Pennsylvania, preached time and time again his great sermon "Come before Winter." Why? Because it reminded the thousands who heard it of their chores of servanthood which needed tending while there was still time.

Once he preached the sermon in Philadelphia. A medical student was present. When the service was over, the student went back to his room where he kept repeating the phrase, "Come before winter." He thought to himself, *I'd better write a letter to my mother.* He wrote the letter, dropped it in a mailbox and returned to his room. A few days later a telegram came: "Come at once. Your mother is dying." He took the train that night and hurried to the family farm home. There he found his mother, still living, with a smile of recognition and satisfaction on her face. Under her pillow was the letter he had written after he had heard Dr. Macartney. Her pain was eased as she faced death.

How quickly we forget our calling to be servants. How absorbed we become in our own self-interests. How insensitive we become to the needs of others while seeking to satisfy our own. Yet what joy, what wholeness of life we bring both to others and to ourselves when we faithfully carry out the attitudes and practices of servanthood. And what joy awaits us when we hear the wonderful words of our Lord, "Well done, good and faithful servant" (Matt. 25:21).

5
Living before a Watching World

Therefore, my dear friends, as you have always obeyed—not only in my presence, but now much more in my absence—continue to work out your salvation with fear and trembling, for it is God who works in you to will and to act according to His good purpose.

Do everything without complaining or arguing, so that you may become blameless and pure, children of God without fault in a crooked and depraved generation, in which you shine like stars in the universe as you hold out the Word of life—in order that I may boast on the day of Christ that I did not run or labor for nothing. But even if I am being poured out like a drink offering on the sacrifice and service coming from your faith, I am glad and rejoice with all of you. So you too should be glad and rejoice with me.

For everyone looks out for his own interests, not those of Jesus Christ (Phil. 2:12-18, 21).

So you're a Christian! Are you? If so, you are front and center on stage. The spotlights cut through the darkened theater. There you are, in the middle, for all to see.

It is to the Christian that Paul speaks. He knows you have a high visibility factor. His words stress both how you should live and what qualities others should see in you.

49

Paul capsulizes his suggestions as to how you should live in the following seemingly contradictory terms: "Therefore, my dear friends, as you have always obeyed—not only in my presence, but now much more in my absence—continue to work out your salvation with fear and trembling, for it is God who works in you to will and to act according to His good purpose" (vv. 12-13).

You say, "But I thought I was saved by grace, not by works (see Eph. 2:8-9). Here I've come to Christ with nothing in my hands. I've admitted my sin. I've placed my simple trust in Him. Then suddenly I'm told to work out my own salvation. What in the world is Paul trying to do to me? This seems like a total inconsistency in his teaching."

There's no need to get uptight about this phrase "work out your salvation with fear and trembling." God is not trying to tie you up in the same knots of bondage from which He has just loosened you. He is writing to you as a Christian, saying simply, "Don't stop halfway, Christian. By My grace you are a whole person. Live in an ongoing way as one whom I love."

It's April. The Boston Marathon once again sports its field of several thousand runners set to go those 26 long miles. Some will finish the race. Others will stumble, feet blistered and tired, giving up part of the way through. Are they all participants in the race? Yes. Filled with vigor and enthusiasm when the starter's gun is fired? Yes. But somewhere along the way the energy, the drive, the determination, the strength, the wind to finish the race is gone. The months of invested time, energy, and money stumble off the track with the weary runners.

How often we've seen this happen. Jack and Mary worked hard, giving vital leadership to a suburban Young Life Club. Seventy or eighty teenagers packed Jack and Mary's living room each Thursday night. Dozens of these eager young people came to trust Jesus Christ. That was eight years ago. It's been three years since Jack and Mary have been active in Christian leadership. Occasionally they go to church. The week-in, week-out pace of Christian living has taken its toll. They've forgotten that no one ever said the Christian life would be a snap.

A Continuous Process

Paul emphatically calls us to work out our salvation. The beautiful Greek word he uses means for us to bring our salvation to completion. It stresses the continuing process which will ultimately be concluded. He begs us not to stop halfway.

This does not mean that we are saving ourselves. He emphatically says, "It is God who works in you to will and to act according to His good purpose" (v. 13). The word he uses here is different. Where on the one hand he is calling us to continue forward, he refers to the whole process of salvation as being the action of God. God's action cannot be frustrated. It continues on to full completion.

How can we coordinate these two apparently contradictory emphases? Let's take another look at the rhythm of God's salvation. First He started the process of restlessness within you, which reminded you of your need of Him. Remember that spiritual hunger? Remember that vacuum of life which could not be filled? Remember how Christ brought you to your senses, calming your restlessness with His peace? Through His action you were saved. And He completes the process, working in you both to will and to work for His good pleasure. The initiative is His. The action which brings you to trust Him is His. The completion of the process is His. Salvation is of God. At the same time you are a participant in this process. God needs you to cooperate with Him.

All human analogies break down. The Calvinist believes that you can never lose your salvation. In the process he sketches a high standard of what it means to really come to Jesus Christ in faith. The Arminian holds that you can lose your salvation. Once saved, not always saved. This age-old theological argument need be only academic to the one who faithfully follows through on the grace available in Jesus Christ.

Perhaps the best illustration would be in the terms of the emancipation of slaves. Congress passed the Emancipation Proclamation. People were no longer in bondage. Freedom was a gift. The question was, would people live as those set free? Paul says, "Don't stop halfway. Keep going. Let what God has begun in you continue to its completion."

What Others Should See

Paul, having called you to live within that exciting tension of applying yourself to the work which God is carrying out in you, lists some qualities which others should see while you stand before the watching world.

Quality 1: forward movement. Ever driven a car that got stuck in first gear? There's a limit to how fast that car will go. You can hear that harsh grinding if you try to cram it into second.

God is at work in you. There's a forward movement. He doesn't want you stuck at the same point you were eight years ago, or three years ago. He doesn't want you perpetually working over the same old struggles in Christian living. He never said it would be an easy life. The Christian life is compared to a battle, a struggle. But you should be winning.

Dr. Louis Evans, Jr. once described how God had worked in his life through a small group process. He explained that he had shared some problems he was facing with this small group. The next month he came back and started all over again, sharing the same set of concerns. Suddenly, one member of the group broke in and said, "Stop, Louie, we heard all that stuff last month. What we want to know is what have you done about it. What's happened in your life since last month? What progress is being made? Let's not just have the same old catalog again." This shook Louis Evans up and made him realize that forward progress should be part of the Christian's experience!

Christianity is not a life in which you are placed in a religious structure and left to vegetate. Christian living by its very definition involves growth. There is a maturing process in which God continues to work in your life, nudging you forward.

Quality 2: fear and trembling. See that spotlight focus in on you? Is there the self-contented air of the long-haul professional? In a sense God wants you to be a professional. Yet I don't think He wants you to be like a veteran, seasoned performer who simply steps out on center stage. Everybody knows that the seasoned performer has gotten his routine down pat. Every gesture is perfectly timed to produce audience response. There's a cool, clinical professionalism which has no place in Christian living. Therefore, it is desirable that you not lose that quality of fear and trembling.

We need to stop and figure out what this means. A few months ago I addressed a church junior high group. Once again that frequent question came up: "What does it mean when the Bible says we should fear God? Are we to be scared of God?"

Not for a moment. He is a God of love. He is sensitive to every need. This fear and trembling to which we are called has two dimensions. First, we are to live in the knowledge that without Him we can do nothing. This is a healthy awe and respect of the Lord. It doesn't push us away from Him. Instead it draws us toward Him in a wholesome dependency. He is our source of strength. He makes possible all that is good in our lives. Second, this fear and trembling expresses our desire not to disappoint the Lord. We want to bring pleasure and glory and honor to the One who gave His life for us.

Quality 3: satisfaction. Perhaps that's not the best word to use. I'm trying to state it in a positive way. Paul says, "Do everything without complaining or arguing" (v. 14). Have you ever been around a murmuring, mumbling, complaining person? Are you one yourself? Some people are never content. They find fault with almost everything.

God's ways are not always easy to understand. Sometimes He has to rough us up in the process of moving us forward. Remember Israel? Were they ever a complaining group! Moses describes the story of their deliverance through the Red Sea (Ex. 14). Then Moses and his sister Miriam sang their song of deliverance to Almighty God (Ex. 15). Three days later, as they continued on their journey, they could not find fresh water. They came to a spring called Marah. The water was bitter. "So the people grumbled against Moses, saying, 'What are we to drink?'" (Ex. 15:24) This was just one of the many times they complained.

Are we grumbling, questioning Christians? Surely we're free to raise our questions, but do they destroy that graciousness of life which shows the world that in Christ there is satisfaction?

Quality 4: purity. God wants the world to see Christians whose lives are clean, different from those who do not know the Saviour.

Paul states this call to purity in these words, "Become blameless and pure, children of God without fault in a crooked and depraved generation" (Phil. 2:13). Because He has saved us by His grace, we are without blame before him. He wants us to continue in a lifestyle which does not stand condemned by the world. He uses the term "blameless." This connotes a sincerity, a purity.

Perhaps this reference is to the sacrificial animals. God wanted the very best from the people. He wants the very best from us. Obviously we can't live pure lives in our own strength. He is the source of victory. In Him we may receive purity.

We tend to shy away from Christian discipline which endeavors to maintain some semblance of purity. So the world witnesses a not-to-dedicated group of people who call themselves Christians.

Quality 5: missionary outreach. Paul calls us to shine as lights in the world. This involves verbal witness. Humanly speaking, we are all God has to work through. Does that register? God has chosen to work through us. That puts a heavy responsibility on us to give a clear-cut witness to the claims of Jesus Christ. That witness is to be backed by the lives we live. In the Sermon on the Mount (Matt. 5), Jesus called us the "light of the world." We are a "city set on a hill." We are not to hide our light. People are watching. We are God's vehicle through whom their lives should be touched.

Quality 6: holding fast the Word of life. This means being faithful to His Word. Even when it appears narrow when we want it to be broad. Even when it's exclusive when we'd desire it to be inclusive. We seek His message for our own lives and for the world today. We accept what the Word of God proclaims. We proclaim it with fearlessness, yet in love and persuasiveness.

Who Is No. 1 in Our Lives?

The world watches us from many vantage points. Often they see us through the superficial image we present. They detect that though we say we're committed to Jesus Christ, we're often committed basically to ourselves. And if they'd take a closer look inside the church fellowship, they might discover this to be too glaringly true.

Paul put his finger right on the spot. He was grateful for the unselfish ministry of Timothy, and could commend him highly because of his servanthood attitudes. But this wasn't true of many other believers. Paul had to exclaim, "I have no one else like him. ... Everyone looks out for his own interests" (Phil. 2:20-21).

Ouch! But how quickly this strikes home, especially in our American culture. Everybody for himself. Look out for No. 1. No one else will!

Paul presents the true Christian lifestyle. Possibly it contrasts with our own and will demand some drastic changes in thinking if we are to look out for the interests of Jesus Christ.

What do we spend the most of our time thinking about? Calculating our future? Trying to pay our bills? Hoping to get ahead in life?

If we could take blank pieces of paper and chart our thoughts, where would they focus? We have sets of personal interests. God is interested in these. The question is, how interested are we in *His* concerns? Is there a mutual interdependence between our interests and His?

Paul was concerned about some Christians who had become caught up in self-interests. Seldom do you hear Paul complain. Imprisoned, with his future uncertain, he wrote to a group of believers he loved in Philippi, telling them that there weren't many people in Rome he could really depend on. There were plenty of Christians. He had numerous friends. But in the final analysis they were interested in their own concerns. Only Timothy and Epaphroditus were willing to be expendable for Jesus Christ.

What are the profiles of our lives? We have some clear-cut options. We have the option of doing nothing for the Lord. We can take all of our discretionary income and reinvest it in our own interests. We can take our time and use it for ourselves. We can take all the abilities God has given us and use them for self-gratification.

There's a second option. It is that of becoming interested in others—in fact, becoming quite generous with others for selfish reasons. Charity can be extremely egocentric.

They were a husband and wife team. They worked well together. They had some money. They pledged it to the church. Then they didn't give as much as they had promised, holding back some for themselves. They wanted the recognition that came with such a pledge. There was some status to be gained. Their names? Ananias and Sapphira! (See Acts 5:1-11.)

There's another option to doing nothing or doing for self. It's doing for Jesus Christ.

Meet three friends: first, Paul—Christ-centeredness marked his life. He wasn't perfect. No one is. Here was a man incarcerated. A death sentence hung over him. What did he do? He expressed the enthusiasm he had in sharing Christ with those around him. He spent an enormous amount of time encouraging fellow believers in churches he had started. He spent time writing letters. Not only that. He took great personal concern for those around him. He expressed his depth of appreciation for friends. He was a big, generous Christ-centered spirit.

Meet Timothy: a generous young man, willing to play second fiddle. Few of us have a spirit generous enough to enable us to be No. 2. No one was closer to Paul. This young man's mother and grandmother were Jewish Christians. His father was Greek. Timothy and Paul traveled together. They were together at Philippi. Then in Thessalonica. And Berea. Together they ministered in Corinth, and in Ephesus. He was with Paul in prison in Rome. He was associated with Paul in the writing of at least five letters. Whenever Paul wanted to get across a personal message to a church and was uncertain that the message would get through by mail, he would send it personally with Timothy. Timothy's one desire was to serve Paul in the name of Jesus Christ.

Meet Epaphroditus: the least familiar of the three. When the church at Philippi heard that Paul was in prison, in their love they took action. They picked one of their members and sent him with a gift for Paul. They intended that Epaphroditus stay in Rome and be Paul's personal attendant. He was willing to take the risk of being the personal servant of a man awaiting trial on a capital charge. While in Rome, Epaphroditus became ill and he almost died. This news got back to Philippi. Paul insisted that Epaphroditus go home. Paul referred to him as one who really gave himself as a brother, fellow worker, and a fellow soldier. Paul urged the Philippian church to "Welcome him in the Lord with great joy, and honor men like him" (Phil. 2:29).

See the difference? Contrast the attitude of Paul, the performance of Timothy, and the words of commendation about Epaphroditus with those hauntingly tragic words, "Everyone looks out for his own interests, not those of Jesus Christ" (v. 21).

Measuring Up

How do we measure up to this higher standard? How can we put the interests of Jesus Christ above our own? It all centers in the concept of stewardship. Everything we are and have is God's. He created us. He has given us every material and spiritual possession. Shouldn't He be involved with what we do with all we have? Stewardship involves three basic dimensions of our lives:

One, our time. God needs us. We are all He has to work through. Granted, He has angels. But His primary vehicle of movement on this earth is through humans who are willing to give Him time. Isn't time about the most precious commodity we own? He wants us to work for Him. He wants us to be persons of prayer. He wants to love through us. All these require a commitment of time.

Another dimension of stewardship is talent. We are somewhat gifted persons. We have abilities which God needs. We might never have thought of ourselves as being talented. We might be scared to death to step up into a pulpit to speak. Maybe we can't sing in the choir. Maybe we don't think we would be too effective as teachers. Yet we have some God-given talents which can be greatly effective in His service.

The church is the body of Jesus Christ. There's that recurring New Testament reference to a body not needing three heads. A body needs a couple of hands, a couple of feet, a couple of ears, and one head, plus all the other intricately technical organs, limbs, and other parts which make us capable of action. We each have specific functions to carry out somewhere in the church of Jesus Christ. Some have the gift of hospitality. They can make people feel at home. That's as important as preaching. Some can use their hands to teach boys and girls crafts and arts in the name of the Lord. We each have gifts. God wants us to use them in the interests of Jesus Christ.

There is the *financial* aspect. As much as we don't like to talk about money, we live in an economy made up of dollar signs. Frankly, I enjoy preaching on tithing. Why? Because it thrills me to see people caught up in the exciting potential of giving 10 percent of their income to the work of Christ.

Money is important. How we use our money is a key to who we are. Our tithe represents our dedication to the cause of Christ.

Let's get practical. If you're not a tither, I challenge you to experiment for six months, starting right now. Choose to what church causes you'll give, then give systematically. You'll soon be enriched by such giving.

But, if you're not a Christian please don't give to any church, or any other Christian cause. God wants you more than He wants your money. It is a natural tendency to become absorbed in your own interests—not those of Jesus Christ. To give financially is not enough. God wants your time and talents also.

There is the *motivational* aspect. Don't give so the watching world will be impressed by your philanthropy. Give because you've committed yourself openly and sincerely to the interests of Jesus Christ. Only such giving and living fully pleases Him and represents Him well in this generation that is just as crooked and depraved as Paul's generation was.

6
Living beyond Yourself

But whatever was to my profit I now consider loss for the sake of Christ. What is more, I consider everything a loss compared to the surpassing greatness of knowing Christ Jesus my Lord, for whose sake I have lost all things. I consider them rubbish, that I may gain Christ and be found in Him, not having a righteousness of my own that comes from the Law, but that which is through faith in Christ—the righteousness that comes from God and is by faith. I want to know Christ and the power of His resurrection and the fellowship of sharing in His sufferings, becoming like Him in His death, and so, somehow, to attain to the resurrection from the dead.

Not that I have already obtained all this, or have already been made perfect, but I press on to take hold of that for which Christ Jesus took hold of me. Brothers, I do not consider myself yet to have taken hold of it. But one thing I do: Forgetting what is behind and straining toward what is ahead, I press on toward the goal to win the prize for which God has called me heavenward in Christ Jesus (Phil. 3:7-14).

If the Apostle Paul could suddenly drop in on our era of evangelical self-improvement conferences and formulas, his testimony about what he had attained via self-improvement, positive thinking, or self-conquering techniques would be quite impressive. Most of us would listen closely to his testimony of personal attainments: "If anyone else thinks he has reasons to put confidence in the flesh, I have more: circumcised on the eighth day, of the people of Israel, of the tribe of Benjamin, a Hebrew of Hebrews; in regard to the Law, a Pharisee; as for zeal, persecuting the church; as for legalistic righteousness, faultless" (vv. 4-6).

Quite a reputation. Quite a list of self-improvements. Who could top that? Please, Paul, will you lead our next seminar? Surely you have recognized qualifications to teach us how to live beyond ourselves. You have discovered success in every area of life to which you have put yourself. You stand out above the ordinary.

Paul's Secret

"Wait a minute! Wait a minute!" Paul exclaims, even rending his clothes in dramatic disapproval of such recognition. He almost has to shout in order to quell the onrush of back-patters. Though he has listed all his attainments, his next paragraph begins with the word every theologian says we must pay particular attention to: "but." That word makes all the difference in what Paul is communicating.

Paul immediately makes it clear that his boasting is only fleshly boasting—a listing of his personal attainments—his pedigree, so to speak. His list was much like the attainments we so often seek, and list as important if we are to be accepted with authority.

Then comes Paul's "but." And this paragraph begins his explanation of how he truly got beyond himself—beyond himself into the will of God. Beyond himself into experiencing the power of Christ in realistic ways. Beyond himself to the realization that he was still reaching out to attain the goals of God in Christ Jesus.

"But whatever was to my profit I now consider loss for the sake of Christ. What is more, I consider everything a loss compared to the surpassing greatness of knowing Christ Jesus my Lord, for whose sake I have lost all things" (vv. 7-8).

Getting to such a point in Christian experience is not easy. We just don't make an emotional leap into such a relationship. Nor do we readily surrender our self-improvements to the will of Christ. Only as we gain a knowledge and understanding of the surpassing greatness of Jesus Christ will we ever relinquish our self-made improvements. Thus, what the humble apostle proclaims will be quite foreign to our lifestyle unless we willingly share Paul's attitude. He honestly, and without any reservation, proclaimed, "I want to know Christ and the power of His resurrection and the fellowship of sharing in His sufferings, becoming like Him in His death, and so, somehow, to attain to the resurrection from the dead" (v. 10).

What more expressive way could he give to anyone seeking to live beyond himself? Surely Paul had discovered the secret. And rather than seeking some new self-development methodology, even within the framework of an evangelical church structure, we need to discover the dynamic of realistic identification with the death and resurrection of Jesus Christ.

Paul described how this identification took place: "I have been crucified with Christ and I no longer live, but Christ lives in me. The life I live in the body, I live by faith in the Son of God, who loved me and gave Himself for me" (Gal. 2:20).

To the Romans he explained, "If we have been united with Him in His death, we will certainly also be united with Him in His resurrection. For we know that our old self was crucified with Him so that the body of sin might be rendered powerless, that we should no longer be slaves to sin" (Rom. 6:5-6). This is the victory that not only overcomes the world, but also frees us from enslavement to ourselves.

Of course, Paul is quick to explain that this isn't a once-for-all act. He didn't suddenly become perfect. Rather he recognized his need for continual and constant identification with both the death and resurrection of Christ. As he described his own continuum, he presents several creative steps on how we can live beyond ourselves.

Facing Up to the Fact You're Not Perfect

Paul wasn't a mealy-mouthed, introverted person. He didn't suffer from any lack of self-confidence. Yet he did have a healthy respect for his own human limitations. He realized that humility was one of the toughest commodities to obtain. He wrote: "Not that I have already obtained all this, or have already been made perfect; but I press on to take hold of that for which Jesus Christ took hold of me. Brothers, I do not consider myself yet to have taken hold of it" (Phil. 3:12-13).

Some of us lean continually on glass crutches, made out of our own self-achievements. Biblical writers warn against putting confidence in what you have been able to attain on your own. It strikes me that many people suffer from a "self-made person" syndrome. The "Horatio Alger mentality," commendable in many respects, has caught hold of some who are committed to the basic capitalistic philosophy. Applying themselves with all diligence to their chosen professions, they have proven themselves to be achievers. Perhaps they've earned a prominent position. Or a lot of money. Or a good marriage partner. They pride themselves in their own achievements. Granted, they are many. But if they've forgotten that "every good and perfect gift is from above" (James 1:17), they've forgotten that it's impossible to really make it on their own. Paul the achiever said, in effect, "I do not consider that I have made it on my own" (Phil. 3:10-12).

There's a big difference between Saul of Tarsus the Pharisee and Paul the apostle, writing years later from prison. The same individual, yes. Early in his life he was a self-made man. He had risen to the top in his chosen religious profession. Then Jesus Christ caught him on the road to Damascus, turned his life around, and gave him an authentic sense of humility.

To be humble hurts at first; the initial awareness comes hard. But the encouraging thing is that you don't need to be surprised by your own failures. A self-made person is constantly on the defensive about his areas of weakness. Paul Tournier, a noted Swiss psychiatrist, says there's a tendency to divide individuals into two categories—those who are strong and those who are weak. Society rewards the strong, and tramples the weak. Somehow we view the strong as healthy, the weak as unhealthy. Tournier emphasizes that both of these views are unbalanced. He writes:

> If weakness leads to a sense of failure, strength too has its
> vicious circle: one must go on being stronger and stronger
> for fear of suffering an even more crushing defeat, and
> this race in strength leads humanity inevitably to general
> collapse. . . . I believe there is a great illusion underlying

both the despair of the weak and the unease of the strong—and the misfortune of both. This great illusion is the very motion that there are two kinds of human beings, the strong and the weak. The truth is that human beings are much more alike than they think. What is different is the external mask, sparkling or disagreeable, their outward reaction, strong or weak. These appearances, however, hide identical inner personality. The external mask, the outward reaction, deceives everybody, the strong as well as the weak. All are weak because all are afraid. They are all afraid of being trampled underfoot. They are all afraid of their inner weakness of being discovered. They all have secret faults; they all have a bad conscience on account of certain acts which they would like to keep covered. They are all afraid of other men and of God, of themselves, of life and of death (*The Strong and the Weak*, Westminster Press, pp. 20-21).

If you are a mature believer in Christ, you understand who you are. You face up to your own imperfections. In fact, the spiritual Christian thinks less of self and constantly places more confidence in the Lord. Living beyond yourself involves facing your limitations.

Living with Your Back to the Past

Paul writes, "But one thing I do, forgetting what is behind." Expansive living involves putting away damaging memories.

This doesn't mean forgetting everything. First, you need to remember before you can start to forget. You need to be selective in those things you choose to forget. You need to remember the style pattern of your past successes. You also have to remember the style patterns of your defeats. Forgetting does not eliminate learning. The mature believer in Christ is one who learns. He becomes educated by his victories. At the same time, he learns from his defeats. True education is remembering what you need to remember, and forgetting all else.

I have a friend who is a senior partner of a large Wall Street legal firm. On several occasions he has shared with me sage advice given to him by his mother during his childhood. She urged him to remember one significant thing each day and forget all the rest. Dismiss the irrelevant; remember the important.

The Christian who is living beyond himself has learned to forget those things which are nonproductive for future creative living.

Knowing What You Should Forget

First, you should forget the bad. Forgetting implies forgiving. You as a believer in Jesus Christ are set free from the garbage which cluttered your past life. All of us need an authentic catharsis—a real cleansing. We all need a ventilation of our lives, refreshed by the Spirit of God.

The German poet Goethe emphasized the optimistic possibilities of forgetting the bad and saying that *the one great truth is not that the past is sullied, but that the future is unsullied.* Catch the upbeat of that statement. Forgetting means a finer memory, a clearing of your mind of those things which could only destroy your creativity.

Second, you need to forget certain positive achievements. This is a tough job. We love to pull out our scrapbooks and read the clippings. We love to luxuriate in the achievements of the past. Granted, we should be able to indulge ourselves in a few whimsical moments, reminiscing. But watch out! Sad is the individual who has only the clippings of the past.

If Paul is saying anything with regard to forgetting, he is warning you as a believer to forget all of the spiritual achievements of the past. Remembering is the best way to backslide. That's the best way to dull your cutting edge. Live with your back to the past.

Keeping Your Eyes on the Right Goals

If you really want to live beyond yourself, you have to aspire to worthy goals. Paul writes: "Brothers, I do not consider myself to have taken hold of it. But one thing I do: Forgetting what is behind and straining toward what is ahead, I press on toward the goal to win the prize for which God has called me heavenward in Christ Jesus" (Phil. 3:13-14).

Are your sights set beyond yourself? Are you reaching for a higher goal? I must admit that although I had great admiration for the few men who reached the summit of Mt. Everest, I also sort of pitied them. Why? Because, in some ways, they had reached the ultimate.

Have you ever seen a person who has set his goals and then reached them? God pity him if he doesn't set new goals and then strive toward them. It's dangerous to sit on top of the world.

What little mountain climbing I've done has been in Switzerland with the aid of cable cars and aerial tramways. I remember the thrill of looking down on the world from the top of the mighty Jungfrau. But, frankly, a more stimulating vista for me was to view the Jungfrau from the halfway mark of a nearby mountain range. There I could look down on the villages below, seeing a panorama of the world from which I had just ascended. I could also look on to the vistas above, at the many mighty peaks. I could see from where I'd come but also look to heights yet to be conquered.

A high calling lends enthusiasm and invigorating excitement to life. To quit reaching is to die. God's work also dies in you. Life is easier when you have no reach. But it's not happier. If you are content to aim low, you will soon get satisfied with yourself and lose the exhilaration which comes from the high calling which can be yours in Christ Jesus.

Have Specific Goals

Have you focused in on specific goals? Have you put any of these goals in writing? I suggest that you jot down, in one sentence, your whole basic purpose for living. The achiever puts his goals down in writing to see them in their proper relationships. He puts first things first establishing proper priorities.

Make sure your goals are worthwhile. Some goals get you nowhere. Other goals make little sense. Some goals are distorted. Others are never properly executed.

A few years ago there was considerable discussion about the book by Richard Bach titled *Jonathan Livingston Seagull,* (Macmillan, p. 15). It was a story about a seagull who aspired to reach heights never reached by seagulls. His goal was to fly with precision, speed, and endurance, at extremely high altitudes. His father cuts him to size by saying, "Don't you forget that the reason you fly is to eat."

It is easy to set as goals things of a lesser nature. It is easy to live a style of life which involves flying to eat—instead of eating to fly! It is easy for physical passions, good as they are, to take over, and eliminate the enormous heights of a greater calling.

I urge you to set the highest goal of all—of realizing the very best Jesus Christ has for your life. Focus in on the Person of the Saviour. Confront His revelation in the Bible. Be able to state, without apology, "For to me to live is Christ." What a difference between your goal and your prize. The goal is to be like Christ—to have His very best for your life. One prize you realize at the end of this life is the assurance that you will be forever with the Lord.

Giving Life Everything You've Got!

Paul says, "I press on" (Phil. 3:12). He uses the term "straining toward what is ahead." Can you think of a more creative style of life? Do your very best. There's nothing wrong with a Christian being an achiever, as long as success is kept in proper balance with humility. Be confident, because you are living with a strength which goes beyond yourself. There's a dynamic in the life that is discontented with the present, striving toward the future, and yet undergirded by a deep contentment that says, "I'm at peace with myself, and with my Lord." You're Christ's person. Give Him everything you've got. Strain your every effort toward being the person He wants you to be. Your highest calling is becoming like Jesus Christ. He can give you exciting potential in every area of Christian expression. Apply yourself, with His help, to being the best marriage partner, the best parent, the best professional you can possibly be. There's no room for halfhearted-ness in this business of serving Christ. The mature Christian is one who blends talent with perspiration.

Nothing worthwhile in life comes without effort. The things of most enduring quality are sometimes the most difficult to achieve. There'll be pain and defeats along the way. There'll be points at which your goals will be frustrated. Sometimes your energies will run low. There will be points when your reach will far exceed your realistic grasp. But God gives you gifts so you can put them to work to become the person He wants you to be.

On my desk are two symbols. Occasionally someone observes their apparent contradictory natures. I deny that fact. One is a rough-hewn olive wood cross, symbolic of the life crucified with Christ. The other is a marble statue of the Greek discus thrower. The one calls for self-denial—the losing of self in the service of God and others. The cross reminds me of my own expendability. It highlights the sacrifice which Jesus Christ made on the cross for me. It shows that I can not save myself. All human effort falls short.

The marble statue alerts me to my responsibility for self-mastery. As I look at that statue, I see every muscle geared to the moment. There's no sense of looking back. There's no wasted energy. There's no thought of the past. There's no excess baggage. All is devoted to immediate excellence in which one reaches the peak of one's ability, with goals even beyond that reach for the prize which lies ahead.

God help you, God help me, to live our lives in the strength of the One whose resurrection sets us free, and whose Spirit empowers us. We *can* live beyond ourselves!

7
Striving for Maturity

All of us who are mature should take such a view of things. And if on some point you think differently, that too God will make clear to you. Only let us live up to what we have already attained. Join with others in following my example, brothers, and take note of those who live according to the pattern we gave you (Phil. 3:15-17).

Paul seemed to take for granted that most of the people in the Philippian church had become mature Christians. He says, "All of us who are mature..." Whether he'd say this to us today, in an era which has a much higher percentage of people claiming to be Christians—and in an era when a much higher percentage have the advantage of being able to read and write—is questionable. Many believers are babes in Christ. They know so little of what the Bible teaches. Often they become touchy when faced with the demands of biblical truth. They take part in church functions on the basis of what they get out of it, especially social satisfactions. Only a small percentage commit themselves to sacrificial involvements. Would Paul say to us, "All of us who are mature..."?

What is maturity? How is it measured in the Christian context? How did Paul determine these Philippians had become mature believers?

A dictionary will give various definitions of maturity: becoming full grown, as plants or animals; fully or highly developed; perfected; fully developed, as a person, a mind, a body, etc.

It's rather easy to give examples from nature. At harvest season vegetables and fruits are fully developed. They have matured throughout the growing season and are ready for harvesting, marketing, and eating. We say a large tree is mature. A pig or steer is mature when it is ready for slaughter.

But when it comes to human maturity, we look beyond physical measurements to the personality. How does this person act and react in life? How does he perform under pressure? What type of response does he make when the status quo of his life is challenged? How does he line up with the norms of society? What is his ability to make moral decisions?

Another facet of maturity is the ability to postpone immediate gratification for the ultimate good. Maturity is the capacity to say no right now so that others will not be hurt later. The mature person is not caught up in the immediate, while neglecting ultimate consequences.

Striving for Christian Maturity

Because our present day meaning of *perfect* (Phil. 3:12) means "being without flaw," we need to take a better translation of the Greek word *teleios*—mature. You and I know that in this life we are not flawless. We can only claim, or adhere to, the perfection of Christ to have right standing with God. Our human nature will always be subject to weaknesses. But this does not say we cannot mature. We have not only great opportunity to develop to full growth, but to great responsibility in the process. We should become models not only to new believers, but to the world around us.

Paul talks about those who are mature taking "such a view of things" (v. 15). This is a flashback to the preceding verses in which he discusses the athletic nature of the Christian life.

From the perspective of the world's value system a good Christian is entitled to wear a lot of badges. He's sort of a spiritual Eagle Scout. Paul had listed all the badges he had worn as a religious person. Yet he said that these amounted to nothing more than a pile of garbage. A true professional athlete views his last season in relationship to this season. He takes pride in previous accomplishments but he refuses to lean on his past victories. He's concerned about this season and brings to it all of the experience gleaned from the past. Paul explained that his life in Christ was not based on his previous humanly inspired religious accomplishments. Instead he committed himself totally to the power and authority of the resurrected Christ. He proclaimed, "I want to know Christ and the power of his Resurrection and the fellowship of sharing in His sufferings" (v. 10). He had matured to this advanced point of understanding and commitment. Now he was pressing on toward the goal to win the prize for which God had called him heavenward in Christ Jesus.

One with a mature understanding of the Christian faith accepts what God has prescribed. The mature Christian knows Christ personally. He identifies with the work of Christ. He is empowered by the Holy Spirit—that resurrection power of Jesus Christ. He shares in His Lord's sufferings, looking forward to his own resurrection to eternal life.

There is something different about a mature Christian. He knows who he is, and he doesn't take Christian matters lightly.

Not long ago I received a phone call from a young man who had been part of a college group my wife Anne and I had led seven years ago. He was a religious young student, but at that time was reluctant to talk about the work of the Holy Spirit in the life of a believer. He seemed to experience a form of godliness, but was resistant to teaching relating to Christian maturity. I'd not seen Kent for more than seven years. Kent had accidentally picked up the rebroadcast of one of my Sunday morning messages on his car radio. This stimulated him to call and tell me how God had been working in his life during the past few years. He apologized for his earlier spiritual resistance to the work of God's Spirit and told how he had come into a much deeper understanding of who Christ is and what He wants to do with his life. He talked about his job, and then said this: "Well, at least that is what my job is called. My real work is raising a Christian family."

Christian maturity involves much more than being unwilling to be content with badges of self-righteousness and being identified theologically with the work of Christ. It also involves being aware that this maturation is continual, realistic, practical. We never fully arrive in this life. We're not complete here. If we think we are, we're in trouble. Supersaint Paul had to admit that he wasn't already perfect. He saw life as a rugged process of discipline which involved actions moving toward maturity.

We live in the tension between receiving God's free gift of salvation, not based on our own works, and then working out our own salvation in an energetic, dedicated Christian lifestyle. Paul proclaimed, "Continue to work out your salvation with fear and trembling" while still being consciously aware that "it is God who works in you to will and to act according to His good purpose" (Phil. 2:12-13).

In case you are inclined to become frustrated by your own imperfections, stop to realize that a major part of the maturation process depends on the direction in which you are moving, and not so much on the completeness of your accomplishments. It is possible to be moving at a rapid speed in the wrong direction. That, of course, isn't maturing. It is possible to be caught up in all kinds of frantic religious activity and be nothing more than a kind of spiritual racer. Alexander Maclaren stated this clearly: "The distance a man has got on his journey is of less consequence than the direction in which his face is turned" (*Expositions of Holy Scripture,* [17 vols., Philippians], Baker Book House).

Which Direction Do You Face?

New Testament writers sometimes call men and women who have many sins "saints." Biblical writers called some people perfect who were loaded with imperfections. This was not because God's standard is low. It's because God has a high ideal of the Christian life. It's important to aspire to that ideal. God is most concerned that your lifestyle has a transparent genuineness which lines up with the Holy Spirit's work and seeks to glorify God.

That's why David comes across as a biblical hero, in contrast with Saul. Compare the two men's lives. Saul did a lot of good things. But he was proud, and pride got in the way of his repentance. Saul was melancholy and driven by pride to despair. How quickly that cloud of depression could have lifted if Saul had simply humbled himself before the Lord.

On the other hand, David—adulterer, murderer—entered into a similar agony of soul. But there was a difference. In his despair he cried out, repenting of his sin, begging God's forgiveness, requesting that God would turn him around and head him in the right direction again. Read David's heart-throbbing prayer: "Against You, You only, have I sinned and done what is evil. . . . Surely You desire truth in the inner parts. . . . Cleanse me with hyssop, and I will be clean. . . . Create in me a pure heart, O God, and renew a steadfast spirit within me. . . . The sacrifices of God are a broken spirit; a broken and contrite heart, O God, You will not despise" (Ps. 51:4-17).

That's maturity!

God is saying, "I want you. I'll take you just as you are. If you have a transparent integrity of heart, I can work with you. Hold steady at your present point of spiritual development and let Me lead you from here." If you are an honest Christian, God will make this plain to you. Your part is not to relax your goals or standards. Press on to the goal for the prize of the high calling of God in Christ. That's Christian maturity.

Can Others Follow You?

Concurrent with the maturation process is the awareness that you are called to be an example. What you do is just as important as what you say. You are in the spotlight. You are called to be models of Jesus Christ. Some people will never see through you to Jesus if your lifestyle is not to His glory. The example you set is crucial.

Paul said, "Join with others in following my example, brothers, and take note of those who live according to the pattern we gave you" (Phil. 3:17). That's pretty brash, isn't it? "Look at me! Do as I do!" Some would call that arrogance. Not really. Paul humbly admitted his weaknesses. He clearly stated that he had not already attained everything there was to attain. This humble statement actually increases his qualifications to be an example. He calls on his fellow-believers to imitate him. But he didn't say this boastfully. Rather, as when he wrote to the Corinthians, he wanted them to follow the leadership of Jesus Christ. He told the Corinthians, "Follow my example, as I follow the example of Christ" (1 Cor. 11:1). He described how the Thessalonians also caught this concept: "You became imitators of us *and of the Lord"* (1 Thes. 1:6, author's italics).

How often have you hid behind your humanity? How often have you said to yourself, "Well, I'm a sinner saved by grace. I'm not perfect. I'm not expected to be!" You may use that as a rationalization to avoid being the person Christ wants you to be. You are either a good example or a bad example of Christianity. You and I need to be open in order to see our wrongs.

Paul tells about those headed for destruction. He contrasts them with those who follow his example. He tells his readers to model after him and after those who model after him, not those who claim to be Christians but are not faithful to their Lord. In other words, watch out for bad examples. "Many live as enemies of the Cross of Christ," Paul warned. "Their destiny is destruction, their god is their stomach, and their glory is in their shame. Their mind is on earthly things" (Phil. 3:18-19).

Three Marks of a Bad Example

One, "their god is their stomach." Human appetites are good in their place. Thank God for basic bodily functions. Hunger must be satisfied. Thirst must be quenched. God has given sexual impulses to be used to His glory, including both propagation of the race and personal fulfillment and pleasure. However, it is possible for appetites to become distorted—letting them run you instead of you running them.

Dr. Louis Evans, Sr., told the story of a woman in Hollywood whose husband was dictatorial. She loved Jesus Christ. He knew she took her Bible seriously. He also knew the Bible taught about wives being subject to the authority of their husbands. He wouldn't go to church, but rather went to baseball games every Sunday. He insisted that his wife stay home and serve a good meal at 11:00 A.M. before he went to the ball park. This way, she couldn't go to church. Dr. Evans counseled this woman, telling her that her husband's god was his belly. She could lovingly tell him her primary commitment was to Jesus Christ. She needed to worship her Lord so she could be a good wife. She would prepare an excellent meal, putting it either in the refrigerator or in the oven, and he could eat whenever he wanted before going to the ball game. As for her, she had a prior responsibility.

Are your appetites running your life? One evening my guest on my television show was Rabbi Abraham Twersky. The topic: alcoholism. This brilliant Jewish psychiatrist emphasized that anyone who was dependent on having a drink at any particular time so as to unwind for dinner, relax to go to sleep at night, or to lubricate a social encounter, was—whether he knew it or not—being controlled by alcohol. Human appetites can dominate by destroying yourself and the example you set for others.

Two, there are those whose "glory is in their shame." This means they take pride in things they should be ashamed of. There's the locker room braggart who tells about his way with women. Vile language marks the vocabulary of some people and becomes their glory. More subtly, pride in human accomplishments, which so often are at the expense of those less privileged, instead of being a glory becomes a shame.

Three, there are those whose "mind is on earthly things." This is another means of self-destruction. J.B. Phillips paraphrases it aptly: "This world is the limit of their horizon" (Phil. 3:19). Can you look beyond this world? Or are you boxed in by the finite? What is important to your life? Make a list. How many items on the list would survive your death? What is important to you now is not ultimately important if it cannot survive for eternity. How far do you see into the future?

Paul was probably talking about the gnostics. These were the intellectualizers of Christianity. They divided things between spirit and matter. Spirit is good. Matter is evil. Everything created is essentially evil. The body is created. Therefore it is evil. Since it is evil, you are free to do with it whatever you like: gluttony, adultery, homosexuality, drunkenness—none of these makes any difference.

They only affect the body. The body does not matter. Gnosticism sounds like modern day hedonism!

Others in Paul's day said that no man could be called complete until he had experienced everything that life had to offer. One should go to the depths of sin, as well as to the heights of nobility. In this way God's grace was even more appreciated.

This is a distortion of how you and I are created to function. It is merely a justification for sinning. Grace becomes liberty. In the process, one gets tied up in knots of bondage.

Paul was really saying, "Live out your creed. Live the Christian life to the fullest. Don't just *think* the Christian life. *Live* it! Don't just *talk* about being a Christian. *Be* a Christian!"

God wants you to live to the fullest. In the process He wants you to set an example for others and say, "Do as I do," not just "Do as I say."

Heavenly Citizens

The setting-your-eyes-in-the-right-direction part of maturity helps you become a good example. Just saying you are going to be a good person doesn't make you a good example. Just trying to be a good person doesn't do it either.

In contrast to a person who has his mind set on earthly things, Paul described another kind. He wrote, "But our citizenship is in heaven. And we eagerly await a Saviour from there, the Lord Jesus Christ who, by the power that enables Him to bring everything under His control, will transform our lowly bodies so that they will be like His glorious body" (Phil. 3:20-21).

Do you have an outlook which sees beyond this world? Are you aware of a citizenship which is more important than your national identity? Philippi was a Roman colony. The Romans were masters at placing their colonies at strategic centers. They commanded the major trade routes. Roman justice was administered. Roman morals were observed. These colonies remained unshakably and unalteringly Roman. So Paul says in effect to the Philippians, "Just as the Roman colonists never forget they belong to Rome, you must never forget you are a citizen of heaven. Your conduct must match your citizenship."

Jesus Christ gives you a new citizenship. He is Lord. This means He is your King. He is in charge. He is the Sovereign Ruler. Sure, you are a citizen of your country. You have responsibilities to the nation where you live. But if you're a Christian your primary citizenship is in heaven. You are a citizen of Christ's commonwealth.

In this relationship, the sovereign God enables you to grow in Christian maturity. He makes you the example He wants you to be through the power of His Spirit's work in your life. He changes your life to make it more fit for eternally dwelling in His presence. He wants you to become more like Jesus Christ and reflect that image to the watching world.

The first paragraph of chapter 4 in the Book of Philippians rightfully belongs as a concluding challenge to these concepts in chapter 3. Paul concludes: "Therefore, my brothers, you whom I love and long for, my joy and crown, that is how you should stand firm in the Lord, dear friends!" (Phil. 4:1)

8
Solving Church Conflicts

I plead with Euodia and I plead with Syntyche to agree with each other in the Lord. Yes, and I ask you, loyal yokefellow, help these women who have contended at my side in the cause of the Gospel, along with Clement and the rest of my fellow workers, whose names are in the Book of Life (Phil. 4:2-3).

Do you have a former friend with whom your relationship has been severed? Do you have a Christian brother or sister from whom you've become estranged? If so, there's no time like the present to take affirmative steps to restore your broken relationship. You need not continue estranged from others. You can do more about it than say it is inevitable that sooner or later relationships deteriorate, or that nothing can be done.

Even Christians Have Quarrels
Euodia and Syntyche loved Jesus Christ. They were active workers in the church at Philippi. They had worked side by side with the Apostle Paul. He suggests that they had accomplished much for the cause of Christ. They were much more than tag-alongs. Paul said they "contended at my side in the cause of the Gospel." They were some of the first active, vocal women in the church, and Paul was glad for their support. He readily commended them for their successful

involvements in expanding the ministry at Philippi.

But something happened that broke their relationship. Maybe it started in a discussion of how to do a job, or what should be emphasized, or who should take the lead in the Philippian church's outreach program. Maybe one was a better speaker than the other and drew a larger following or got more compliments. Anyway, they began to quarrel. Earlier in his letter, Paul instructed the Philippians to "do nothing out of selfish ambition or vain conceit" (2:3). Here he might have been personalizing this concept for Euodia and Syntyche.

We're not certain just what the issue was. Their faithfulness to Jesus did not protect them from an interpersonal breach. This is a warning to us. Jealousies, frictions, differences of opinion can creep into a church's fellowship. And before these develop into broken Christian relationships, they must be dealt with in love and patient understanding.

Unfortunately, many churches seem to be good breeding places for quarrelsome relationships. One rather famous preacher recently stated that the best advice his father gave him was to always have some controversy going! How contrary to the Spirit of Jesus Christ and the instruction of the great apostle.

The more intense the people of a church become in seeking to advance the cause of the Gospel, it seems that the more chance differences and possibly quarrels will be produced.

You say, "Impossible!" What I mean is this. A cold, formal nonspiritual church is much less apt to stimulate broken relationships among people. The potential for differences increases when people take their faith seriously. It's difficult to get into an argument with someone who doesn't care about anything, unless that person simply wants to argue. A lukewarm Christian doesn't upset many people. That is, unless he has succumbed to a lackadaisical obstinacy which is a result of his spiritual laziness.

A church is like a family. In fact, it is a family. When my kid sister and I had our fights, we knew each other's vulnerable points. We would attack at the spot of deepest feeling, at the point where the other was most sensitive. Of course, we loved each other. We played together. Did things together. Shared our dreams. Yet it seemed the closer we became, the more vulnerable we were to little hurts. Those subtle barbs. We had our times of broken relationships, made all the more painful because we loved each other.

So don't be surprised if you see trouble in the church. When members of the family of God become intensely involved with each other, they become more easily hurt. This is mainly because they open themselves more and more to one another with each taking seriously the business of serving Jesus Christ within the community of relationships. But in all human relationships the old human nature can crop up, bringing pain. Often the most active members get out of sorts with each other.

I'll never forget that deacons' meeting. It happened several years ago. The 12 men gathered to discuss the physical well-being of their church. Each of these men loved the Lord. Each had a high degree of loyalty to the fellowship. Each wanted to be a good steward of the church building. Yet each had a slightly different understanding of what that stewardship should be. For the life of me, I can't remember the particular topic discussed. But I do remember how the conversation began to heat up. Emotions came to the surface. Suddenly one deacon jumped out of his chair, lunged across the room at another, and challenged him to a fistfight. The rest of us were stunned! Finally we got our irate brother calmed down. These two men were like Euodia and Syntyche. They had literally "labored side by side in the Gospel." They knew each other well. Yet, some small frictions caused sparks to develop—and suddenly produce an explosion!

I was deeply bothered by this outburst until I had some time to reflect. It dawned on me that this explosion had taken place because each had made a great commitment to the church. I could name others whose blood pressure wouldn't have risen a fraction in any discussion of church business. Why? Because they didn't care what happened. They weren't really committed. That was not their life. Where there is greater commitment, there is greater potential for the hurt of broken relationships. When zeal is intensified, so may be the impact of disagreement.

Often the differences are legitimate. No two people think exactly the same. Family backgrounds influence our responses. We are products of our cultures. Ideologically, no two people are identical. We are gifted with distinct emotional equipment which can serve us well or serve us poorly. Hurts over little things, which are allowed to fester, can destroy relationships.

Paul doesn't tell us what the issue was. It makes no difference. We do know that Euodia and Syntyche quarreled. Two fine Christian women had come to a disagreement. Paul desperately desired that their relationship be restored.

Do you have a broken relationship with someone? Do you avoid another's glance? Have you been hurt by somebody's words? Even the most sincere Christians can quarrel.

Something Should Be Done

It's not God's will for you to keep a broken relationship, even though there may seem a very good reason for doing so. A quarreling church, a quarreling family, or quarreling individuals detract from the glory due to the Lord Jesus. Paul urged the two feuding women to "agree with each other in the Lord," to be of the same mind.

We're not talking about being rubber stamps. God has no place for "cookie-cutter Christians" who all look and act alike. You have your gifts—your unique abilities given by God—and I have mine. At the same time, there is to be unity of spirit among believers. The Scriptures are clear on this.

Paul exhorts us to stand together in unity: "I appeal to you, brothers, in the name of our Lord Jesus Christ, that all of you agree with one another so that there may be no divisions among you and that you may be perfectly united in mind and thought" (1 Cor. 1:10).

Paul had gotten word that there was quarreling in the church at Corinth. Division had taken place. Some looked to one teacher. Others liked another. Some preferred the old pastor; some the new. Some prided themselves on being above any petty human attachments. The proud elitists said they followed only Christ Himself.

The Apostle John quoted Jesus' desire that the church stand united. "My prayer is not for them alone. I pray also for those who will believe in Me through their message, that all of them may be one, Father, just as You are in Me and I am in You. May they also be in Us, so that the world may believe that You have sent Me" (John 17:20-21).

James instructs us not to be caught up in strife. "But if you harbor bitter envy and selfish ambition in your hearts, do not boast about it or deny the truth. Such 'wisdom' does not come down from heaven but is earthly, unspiritual, of the devil. For where you have envy and selfish ambition, there you find disorder and every evil practice" (James 3:14-16).

To Timothy, Paul wrote, "The Lord's servant must not quarrel; instead, he must be kind to everyone, able to teach, not resentful. Those who oppose him he must gently instruct, in the hope that God will grant them repentance leading them to a knowledge of the truth" (2 Tim. 2:24-25).

The writer of the Book of Proverbs is quite blunt: "He who loves a quarrel loves sin" (Prov. 17:19).

This does not mean that we should water down our convictions. Sad is the church in which strong biblical concerns take second place to a sentimental spirit of unity. We are not to accommodate worldliness. Consensus or common denominator theology must be rooted out, as we put a top priority on biblical faith. Unfortunately, sometimes we mistake our own human irritability for conviction. We alienate our true loved ones in a way which is inexcusable. We enjoy fighting.

Straightening Things Out

First, we need to humble ourselves. We talk about Jesus identifying with us. He crawled into human flesh to get the feel of how we live. Have you tried to get inside a person who gives you a hard time? Are you able to see why he thinks and acts the way he does? Have you identified with the dynamic of his temperament? His family background? His upbringing and schooling? Or have you triggered negative reactions on his part?

You'll never restore relationships if you are not willing to take a healthy share of the blame. You may be technically right, but your attitude is wrong. Or your attitude may be right, but you may be technically wrong. Paul didn't try to fix the blame on either Euodia or

Syntyche. His desire was to see that the broken relationship was restored. He wasn't about to waste his time or energy arguing about blame.

It takes two to have a fight. Have you ever tried to goad someone into a fight who refused? Frustrating, isn't it? He won't play the game so there can't be any battle. On the other hand, you find some people who seem to enjoy fighting. They diligently defend their prejudices.

It takes the work of the grace of God in your life to humble yourself so you can see where you are wrong. Only when you are willing to take a healthy share of the blame can the stage be set for reconciliation.

Second, we need to apologize. Straight and simple. It isn't easy to go to an estranged friend and say, "I'm sorry."

How often holiday seasons become marred by misunderstandings! Your college student returns home—usually at Christmas. You've waited eagerly for your child to return, but when he gets home all you seem to do is argue. Within a few hours, what you had hoped to be a beautiful celebration is spent in a spirit of antagonism and quarreling. Possibly you are affronted by the challenges your collegian presents to your traditional beliefs and practices. You wanted him to expand his views of life in college, but you aren't prepared for the direction he has chosen. And though you said you respected his individuality, you really and secretly hoped he'd follow your beliefs and lifestyle— almost totally!

The sooner you realize that it's this individual uniqueness before God which creates the potential for disharmony, the more quickly you will be able to resolve differences. The sooner you realize that what you're enduring is natural at this stage of life, the more freely you will be able to embrace each other. You can accept each other even though you stand at different points of spiritual development. For a parent not to be firm in his faith through years of Christian experience would indicate something is wrong. For a young person not to be raising some legitimate questions, something would also be wrong. What you need to do is go to each other. Throw your arms around the one you've hurt through either your inflexibility or prideful arrogance. Take the initiative. A whole new day will dawn in your relationship. It won't be the last time you'll have to say you're sorry or to make amends. But it will be a great moment of liberation in Christ!

Third, be willing to forgive, no matter how many times you've been injured by that same person. So often you and I put a limit on our forgiveness. Peter asked Christ how many times a person should forgive someone who sinned against him. "Up to seven times?"

Jesus answered, "I tell you, not 7 times, but 77 times" or as the *King James Version* puts it, "70 times 7" (Matt. 18:22).

Then Jesus told the story about a king who wished to settle accounts with his servants. One was brought in who owed the king the equivalent of many thousands of dollars. The king ordered him to be sold into slavery, along with his wife and children, so that the payment could be made. The servant fell on his knees before the king, pleading for patience. Suddenly the king, touched with pity, released him and forgave his entire debt.

Then the same servant turned around, and met a fellow-servant who owed him a very small amount of money. Seizing him by the throat, he demanded: "Pay me what you owe. Right now!" The fellow-servant fell down, begging for patience. It was refused. The forgiven servant threw his debtor into prison.

Word got back to the king. He was furious. Calling the formerly forgiven servant before him, he angrily denounced him for not showing the same mercy to his fellow-servant which he had received. Withdrawing his pardon, the king had this first servant thrown into jail. Jesus said, "This is how My heavenly Father will treat each of you unless you forgive your brother from your heart" (Matt. 18:35).

We are to forgive an infinite number of times. You would lose count of how many times you'd forgiven the same person if you'd shoot for the 70 times 7. Nor does God count the number of times He forgives you, or say, "All right, this is the last time." God wants you to apply the same infinite forgiveness to others.

God also wants you to forgive even when the other person doesn't recognize his wrong. That's difficult. It galls us to offer forgiveness to a person who won't admit he's wrong. You know he's wrong. He's caused you considerable pain. But he won't own up to his wrongness.

"You mean I should forgive that person?" That's the best way to restore the relationship. Forgive him and cancel the debt.

Jamie Buckingham tells about a bad debt he had. He had loaned a friend $400. The friend insisted on signing a note with interest which read, "On or before May 1, I agree . . ." Long before May 1 rolled around, his friend and his family had rolled out of town. A year later, Buckingham wrote him a letter saying, "Forget the interest and just pay the principal." His friend wrote back that business was bad, but he was due a bonus at the end of the month. He would pay then. Another year went by; still Buckingham heard nothing. Two years passed.

Buckingham described how the situation began to eat away at him: "Sometimes at night I would lie awake thinking about how to get my money back. My blood would boil." Then one day it dawned on him that though the bad debt obviously wasn't affecting his friend, it was tearing him to pieces. "Slowly I became aware of the spiritual damage it was doing as I stewed in my resentment and bitterness. Instead of feeling such seething reaction, I knew I should be praying for my nonpaying friend, but it was impossible. All I wanted to do was choke him until he spat out the money. And not only that, I found myself wanting to choke a lot of other people who had wronged me."

Buckingham began to read the Bible. He discovered scores of passages on forgiveness. He saw that God wouldn't forgive him as long as he held an unforgiving spirit against others. Finally, under conviction, he dug into his file cabinet and pulled out the four-year-old note. He wrote across the bottom: "Paid in full for Jesus Christ's sake. Ephesians 4:32." Then he mailed the note in an unmarked envelope to his debtor friend.

He describes the heavy weight that lifted from his mind. "Since my friend no longer owed me money, I could love him again. And my channel of love to others has been unplugged also!" (*Guideposts,* April 1974, p. 20-21)

What a great way to restore a broken relationship!

Humble yourself to see where you have been wrong. Apologize. Be willing to forgive.

What letter should you write? What phone call should you make?

What visit should you make? Start immediately to demonstrate the reconciling love of Jesus Christ.

9
Practicing Rejoicing

Finally, my brothers, rejoice in the Lord! It is no trouble for me to write the same things to you again, and it is a safeguard for you.

Rejoice in the Lord always. I will say it again: Rejoice! Let your gentleness be evident to all. The Lord is near. Do not be anxious about anything, but in everything, by prayer and petition, with thanksgiving, present your requests to God (Phil. 3:1; 4:4-6).

A good teacher exhibits three basic qualities: first—a desire for his students' welfare; second—willingness to repeat time and time again what is important; third—patience in allowing the student enough time to learn his lesson. Paul demonstrated these qualities. He was concerned with the spiritual welfare of fellow believers. He was willing to repeat messages of importance constantly. Repetition is good pedagogy. As human beings, we crave novelty—to hear something new. Our ears itch for clever words, but what we really need is stable, basic teachings. Patiently Paul kept repeating the same message, calling believers to rejoice in the Lord, and coupled with that call he gave practical insights into how to rejoice.

Beware of Joy Thieves!
If you want to rejoice in the Lord, watch out for those who would steal your joy.

Paul was followed everywhere by Jewish zealots who tried to deprogram his converts. Men and women came alive in Jesus Christ and their lives were changed. A new joy, a fullness of life, and a sense of well-being took over.

But Satan doesn't want you happy in the Lord. He'd much prefer to strip you of your spiritual enthusiasm. He walks along many different avenues. Sometimes he uses people to detour your spiritual progress. Paul gave this warning: "Watch out for those dogs, those men who do evil, those mutilators of the flesh" (Phil. 3:2). Strong labels, aren't they? God doesn't want you seduced into a wrong lifestyle which negates what He is doing in you.

In our country we keep dogs as pets. That has not always been the case. In the time of Jesus, dogs were roaming street animals. They traveled in packs, often hunting through garbage dumps and rubbish heaps. They were a snapping, nasty, snarling group. They had no owners. Feeding on filth, those diseased animals often attacked passers-by. In Bible times a dog represented a low life.

Jesus painted a picture of the rich man and Lazarus. Lazarus found increased torture in his sickness and poverty, as the street dogs came and licked his sores.

The Old Testament law compared the price of a dog with a prostitute. Money earned from selling a dog or earned from the sale of sexual favors was not acceptable to God.

Within the Jewish context which looked down on dogs, Paul referred to these overly zealous protectors of Jewish traditions as the very lowest type of life, using words with which the Jews were familiar. Likewise, you should watch out for anyone who would take away from you the joy which is yours in Jesus Christ.

These evil workers in Paul's day showed enormous religious zeal. But it's not enough to be enthusiastic and sincere; you need to be correct. Religious practices can be important. However, they are not the essence of joy-giving faith.

What can be an outward sign of an inner work of God's grace can also be just an outward sign for the sake of display. This is what happened to the God-given practice of circumcision. The Jews took pride in their religious trappings. Each Jewish male bore a mark on his body—a symbol of his covenant with God. Pride in that mark instead of God's covenant twisted what was good into something destructive. Ordained by the Lord, it became simply a mutilation of the flesh, as religious zealots prided themselves in a form of godliness which denied the power of God.

There are those today who would steal your joy in the Lord. Some would force you, even after you receive salvation by grace, to live according to a legalistic system. Others would set up their own experience as the norm for all believers. This can happen in relation to the use of spiritual gifts. For several years a young lady had heard about the gift of tongues. Some friends had tried to convince her that this was the ultimate in Christian experience. In the process of seeking this gift, she began to lose the joy of the Lord which had been hers since conversion. She was in agony. Then a group of her friends took part in laying on of hands and prayed that she'd receive this gift. Nothing happened. Reluctantly, she concluded that an experience of speaking in tongues was not God's will for her life. Gradually, her joy in the Lord was restored. How many people like her have lost their joy because of the well-meaning, over-enthusiastic witness of those who universalize their own experiences beyond biblical normalities and examples.

Earning Your Stripes

Badges don't count for much. They don't bring a lasting joy. But somehow people transfer the system of awards into the spiritual area of their lives.

Were you ever a Cub Scout? If so, you may have worked hard to become a Bobcat, then a Wolf, then a Bear. Remember how your mother sewed those badges on your blue shirt? What pride you took in them!

Or maybe you worked hard to become an officer in the military. Finally, you received your bars. It was a day of celebration and great joy. The metal brought joy. It represented accomplishment. It hadn't come easy. A high price was paid for that day of recognition. You sat there admiring your beautifully decorated new uniform.

Now what do you do? Spend the rest of your life sitting there admiring your uniform? No. The bars on your shoulders are only an outward adornment that recognizes your accomplishment.

Christianity is different from every other religion. You are awarded God's grace not on the basis of year in, year out accomplishment. You are given it as a free gift. You earn your bars not because of years of faithful service—but because your Commander in Chief loves you and desires to bestow honor on you. Paul described the distinction between those who simply circumcised the flesh—finding in that their religious identity—and those who were the true circumcision. "For it is we who are the circumcision, we who worship by the Spirit of God, who glory in Christ Jesus, and who put no confidence in the flesh" (Phil. 3:3).

Where is your confidence? In your accomplishments? In some religious affiliation? In the inheritance of someone else's decision for Christ? Or is it in a deep working of God's Spirit in you?

The joyful Christian is one who gets beyond awards. His is not the circumcision of the body. Even in true Old Testament spirituality it was called the circumcision of the heart (Deut. 10:16).

When Jesus spoke to the woman at the well, outside the village of Sychar, they looked toward Mount Gerizim which was a physical symbol of her Samaritan faith. But Jesus used terms that went beyond outward symbols. To her He talked about God as Father, about true worship in spirit and in truth. He talked about a change of heart, and a refreshing, Living Water which could quench her inner spiritual thirst in a way that no attachment to external religious symbols could ever do. She wasn't a pagan. She was a highly religious person, but her personal life was messed up. She could talk the language, but Jesus knew she lacked the true joy (John 4:1-26).

Paul illustrated this fact, giving a rundown from his own experience. He said, "I've got a lot of badges. If this is where the action is, count me in. I can boast more than anyone else. I was circumcised when I was eight days old. I am one of the people of Israel who can trace his origin back to Abraham. I am an Israelite of the tribe of Benjamin. Talk about being elite. I'm elite. Out of my tribe came the first king of Israel. In fact, my name used to be Saul, as his was. I belong to the aristocracy, and I'm a Hebrew of the Hebrews. My family has stubbornly refused to be assimilated among the nations. I am a pure blood Jew. I still speak the Hebrew tongue, though I was born and raised in the Gentile city of Tarsus. Talk about badges—I've got them. I was in the group of the spiritual athletes of Judaism who were the separated ones, determined to keep the Law in every detail. Not only that, I was also a true defender of the faith. I persecuted the church of Jesus Christ. I tried to wipe out those opponents of Judaism. If obeying the old Law made one righteous, I was righteous" (author's paraphrase of Phil. 3:5-6).

Then Paul says, "But whatever was to my profit I now consider loss for the sake of Christ. What is more, I consider everything a loss compared to the surpassing greatness of knowing Christ Jesus my Lord" (Phil. 3:7-8). Paul considered all the badges as meaningless. Only God's acceptance and forgiveness produced true joy in his final analysis.

An Unusual Joy

In his description of joy, Paul gave a personal testimony. He was quick to say there was something better than having all the status symbols of religion. He was disowned by the same group that had made him proud. But he was now in Christ, which was far better. Christ became the source of his true happiness.

First, the fulfillment of joy is to know Jesus Christ. To "know" often conjures up intellectual acknowledgment. But this knowledge goes much deeper. It describes an intimacy of relationship which penetrates beyond a superficial knowing *about*. It involves commitment of life to that person, a lifestyle of closeness.

Second, joy comes from knowing Christ and the power of His resurrection. There is power, a spiritual dynamic, resulting from Christ's victory over death. Your sins are forgiven. His Spirit is with you. He energizes you. You don't have to go through life on your own. An inner strength refreshes you when your strength is gone.

It is heartbreaking to stand by the side of a battered, broken person—someone who has come to the end of his own resources and has nowhere to turn. Whether it be pride that won't let him turn to Christ, or simply ignorance of the available power, he's a sad, joyless person. Joy comes from spiritual energy. Spiritual energy comes from the Holy Spirit.

Third, real joy involves sharing in Christ's suffering, and becoming like Him in His death. We shy away from difficulty—and often miss the joy that can come from tough times. When ruggedness or difficulty come our way, we often resent our pains. But the Apostle Paul says that to suffer for our faith is a privilege, not a penalty. There's joy in paying a price for something worthwhile—something that produces maturity.

Fourth, joy leads to attaining the resurrection from the dead. Paul doesn't express doubt about this. Instead he rejoices over the fact that Christ has promised that you will spend eternity with Him. You have life with Christ in heaven to look forward to. Can you think of anything better?

One day's mail brought a most fascinating little announcement. At first glance, it looked like a wedding invitation. How stunned Anne and I were to read:

A Fellowship of the Resurrection
meets for
a Service of Praise and Thanksgiving
for Christ's victory over death and
in loving memory of _____ .

Our dear friend had gone to be with Christ. It wasn't to be a mournful funeral, but a joyous participation in Christ's—and his— resurrection!

Joy Brings Thanksgiving

Are you aware that instead of anxiety, your life can be marked by the qualities of joy and magnanimity? The apostle wrote: "I will say it again: Rejoice!" (Phil. 4:4) This sounds like a pretty optimistic approach to life. Rejoice. Have a life full of joy.

You would think that the apostle was writing a thanksgiving message during a time of personal prosperity. But this was far from true. Almost certain death awaited him as he sat in prison dictating these words. And these same words were addressed to Philippian Christians who were about to face bitter persecution. Paul was sharing an eternal invitation to joy—a joy that has its source in the personal presence of Christ.

Not only can your life be marked by joy, but it can also be marked by a quality of *magnanimity*. That's not exactly the word Paul used. He wrote, "Let your gentleness be evident to all." There's really no word in English that fully captures what Paul had in mind. Some translators have substituted "patience," "softness," "honesty," and "forbearance" for *gentleness*. Another renders it, "Let the world know you'll meet them halfway." The true meaning is that the Christian life is more than rules and regulations. Jesus Christ can transform your life by the love of God. In the process He wants to sensitize you into showing compassionate and tender love toward others. The gentleness which Paul referred to involved having a big spirit toward others. William Barclay explains this quality as "gracious gentleness."

If you are a Christian, you know there's something involved in living beyond the ideas of justice and fair play. God has forgiven you in Jesus Christ. He wants to release you from the bondage of negative, rule-book living, into a positive upthrust of the joy and magnanimity that gives others the benefit of the doubt.

How to Rejoice

You say, "This all sounds good, but how do I rejoice with all my problems? How can I live a magnanimous life toward others?"

Consider first, "The Lord is near." This simply means you don't have to manufacture joy or magnanimity. Jesus Christ is present every minute of your life. If you trust Him, you can benefit from His presence. He will give you His Spirit so you can maintain constant and meaningful fellowship with Him.

Are you living as if the Lord is near? Or are you walking through life out of touch with the reality of His presence?

In addition to reminding yourself that the Lord is at hand, Paul suggests something more: "Do not be anxious about anything, but in everything, by prayer and petition, with thanksgiving, present your requests to God" (Phil. 4:6).

Paul urges you to pray. The Christian life is not a spiritual narcotic.

It calls for an active, responsive, aggressive lifestyle. You can pray about everything. Let your requests be made known unto God. Imagine that He's like a loving parent, close at hand. He will *always* listen to you. He will provide the antidote to anxiety. Anxiety lets up when you know that the God who created you stands by your side in personal love and tenderness.

Thankful in Everything

Not only does Paul call you to a spirit of joy and magnanimity. Not only does he remind you that Jesus Christ is near and wants your prayers. He also has a little phrase that can completely revolutionize your lifestyle. He writes, "In *everything,* by prayer and petition, *with thanksgiving,* present your requests to God" (Phil. 4:6; author's italics).

Your whole lifestyle should be one of thanks implying total submission to Jesus Christ. This is the essence of Christianity. Paul challenged the Ephesians to be "always giving thanks to God the Father for everything, in the name of our Lord Jesus Christ" (Eph. 5:20). He said that giving thanks was the will of God for each Christian: "Give thanks in all circumstances, for this is God's will for you in Christ Jesus" (1 Thes. 5:18).

Are you thankful in everything?

This means being *thankful for all good things.* Are you concentrating on them? We do on Thanksgiving Day. But Paul tells us to be thankful 365 days of the year—for family, friends, health, God, all material things. It's not difficult to be thankful for these things, but we sometimes forget to express appreciation.

Let me suggest another type of thanksgiving—an attitude of *thankfulness for the lack of bad things.* Seven years ago I severely sprained my ankle. All I could think about was the pain. I would have given anything for relief. Several years prior to the sprained ankle, I had been running on the beach and put a rusty spike through my bare foot. I would have given anything to have been spared the pain. Remembering those pains, it's still hard for me to be thankful that right now I'm free from any excess physical pain. That's what I'm talking about. Remember the last cold you had? The last financial crisis? That marital upset? That loss of job? Perhaps you have some of these things bogging you down now. But you don't have everything going wrong at once. Thank God for the lack of bad things in your life, instead of spending all your time fretting about one or two negatives.

"Be thankful in everything" doesn't mean just good things or the lack of bad things. It also means being *thankful for those things that are not so good.* Here's where the rub comes. Isn't it a little bit idealistic for the Word of God to instruct you to be thankful in everything—even the bad things in life?

How about criticism? Are you thankful for criticism and for your critics? I don't like it when criticism nails me to the wall when I'm truly trying to do my best. Do you?

Things may be bad for you in the area of family finances. Do your best to counteract it and think of a possible fringe benefit. Your children may come out of this stronger as a result of discovering that they have to earn money on their own, and not depend on the affluence of Mom and Dad. They mature and you can give thanks.

Perhaps it's poor health that is strangling you. In your gloomy position of life, how can you be thankful? I'll never forget Dr. V. Raymond Edman, past president of Wheaton College, a scholar, administrator, and deeply spiritual man of God. In the later days of his life, he was plagued by physical blindness. While serving as college president, he was absent for weeks at a time, lying immobile in a hospital bed. His head was cushioned in sandbags as he recovered from surgery for a detached retina. Dr. Edman would come back and share that even in those long periods of physical darkness, thanksgiving was possible because the Lord was so close at hand.

Dr. Paul E. Parker tells how a prolonged illness caused him anxiety and depression. Early one morning he awoke with a slight fever, sore throat, runny nose—all symptoms of a cold, or at worst, a light case of the flu. But for three weeks these symptoms continued, with no appreciable change. Finally he submitted to the same tests he had so often prescribed for others. His doctor took one look at the results: hepatitis. Nothing but bed rest for several months.

Feelings of frustration swept over him. Would the Lord help him cope? He had heard that many of life's greatest lessons come in the crucible of suffering. But to him this had been just a pious platitude. Now it became a ringing reality. Set aside from an active practice, he reached out to the Bible. "In everything give thanks." *Really? In everything?* "God, thank You for hepatitis. I don't enjoy it; I don't like it, but there must be a purpose in it—Your purpose. So I thank You for it."

And so on down the line: "Thank You for the nausea; for the severe headaches; the fever." Each step of faith seemed traumatic. Accepting his reactions as normal, he began to accept his condition—to treat every period of anxiety and depression as an object. Each object he turned over to the Lord. And he discovered prayer again. His busy schedule had not given him enough time for Bible reading and prayer. Now he could saturate his mind with the Word of God. Now he could talk calmly with the Lord. No rush. Finally, he could laugh at the clock and the slavery with which it had bound him. By developing a spirit of thankfulness for even his bad experiences, Dr. Parker validated God's faithfulness.

What's bad in your life? Be thankful in everything. Not just a fatalistic thankfulness, but a buoyant confidence that God is at work and will never let you down or do you harm.

The Results

The result of this whole business is peace. What do you want more than peace? God promises, "The peace of God, which transcends all understanding, will guard your hearts and your minds in Christ Jesus" (Phil. 4:7). You say, "What do you, a rather young minister, leading a rather sheltered, charmed life, know about peace in the midst of suffering?" Probably not as much as some do—or as much as I will someday. Yet I can say from my modest years of experience, marked with my own share of troubles, that God is faithful. His peace does transcend all human understanding.

Fortunately, the authority of this message does not rest on the experience of a preacher. It rests on the authority of God's Word. It finds its ultimate vindication in the long-haul, personal experience of suffering as you, day in and day out, discover Jesus Christ is all He claims to be. There is no need for anxiety. Instead of somehow conning yourself into believing everything will work out all right, you can have the objective confidence of God's presence in Jesus Christ. He is who He claims to be. You can put your trust in Him!

10
Thought-
Conditioning

Finally, brothers, whatever is true, whatever is noble, whatever is right, whatever is pure, whatever is lovely, whatever is admirable—if anything is excellent or praiseworthy—think about such things. Whatever you have learned or received or heard from me, or seen in me—put it into practice. And the God of peace will be with you (Phil. 4:8-9).

You are in the process of becoming what you are thinking about. Your thoughts determine your life. What you think; you are. "For as he thinketh in his heart, so is he" (Prov. 23:7, KJV). This means that if you think about something long enough, you become strongly influenced by it.

It's a gripping holiday network production of "Scrooge." Hosted by the Spirit of Christmas Past, Scrooge and the viewer observe this selfish man's early life. First he's a sensitive boy with great potential. He is playing with his sister, caught up in holiday fun. Soon he becomes a young man entering into business. He and his fiancée show beautiful love for each other.

The production shows Scrooge going back and forth—first to his desk to work on his accounts—then with her on a picnic. Again he's back at his desk. Months fly by. More time is spent in business. Fewer

97

hours are spent with his fiancée. He bombards his mind with aspirations of profit-making. Ledgers dominate his time and thinking. Less and less time is available for his sweetheart and nonbusiness activities.

One day she bursts through his office door. With eloquent perception she accuses him of having a new lover. Brokenhearted, she flings her engagement ring on his desk, promising never to bother him again. She turns and departs, closing the door swiftly behind her. From his second-story window he watches her walk down the narrow London street, and out of his life forever. Slowly he turns to his desk. Gently he places the ring in a drawer. Scrooge has chosen his true love. It's money. Though it's early in his life, we can easily anticipate what his lifelong priority will be.

If you think about something long enough, you will be severely influenced by it. Your mind will settle into a groove. Much of what you are and much of your influence on others is the result of your thought-conditioning. Don't be like Scrooge. Don't become "the kind of man who is always thinking about the cost" (Prov. 3:7). Don't let money become your true love.

He was in his early 40s—a department store executive Out-of-town travel was essential. He missed his wife and three children. Idle evenings in big cities became unbearable. At one time he would never have thought of entering pornographic shops. At home he had been part of a movement to close them. But his curiosity got the better of him. He spent one evening in New York browsing in a porno place, nervously wondering if anyone would recognize him. Active churchgoer. Religious person. He went back to his hotel room feeling guilty. The next time it was easier. The pattern was established. The more perverted, the more exciting. This increasingly steady diet was having its subtle, debilitating effect. It was bringing about spiritual strangulation. No longer was the Bible appealing. No longer did prayer have its place. Temptation toward dirty literature gave way to fantasy. Fantasy gave way to practice. This intellectual infidelity was followed by a series of one night stands on the road. His hunger could not be satiated. Never intending this, he had thought-conditioned himself to moral destruction.

Think on These Things

Paul sketches an alternative lifestyle. Knowing the importance of thought-conditioning, he urges believers to flood their minds with that which is good. He gives several ways to properly condition the mind. "Finally brothers, whatever is true, whatever is noble, whatever is right, whatever is pure, whatever is lovely, whatever is admirable—if anything is excellent or praiseworthy—think about such things" (Phil. 4:8).

This is positive, spiritual thought-conditioning. It's a call to bombard your mind with constructive thoughts. Do you want to stabilize yourself against the subtle encroachments of sin? Try these six suggestions:

1. *Think about whatever is true.* It's easy to mistake error for truth. It's possible to be a well-meaning person, yet function by rules and convictions which are entirely wrong. The day after his Watergate conviction, John Ehrlichman was asked what he would do differently if he could relive the last several years. He voiced his whimsical musings about the past. If he could do it all over again, he would have been more of a moral conscience to the President. He would have said, "Mr. President, you have that alternative. But it is wrong!" Instead, by silence, he and his colleagues—fearful of the truth—covered lie upon lie, bringing themselves and all they cherished to tragic disrepute.

Is it true? There is no substitute for integrity. Is it true? Again and again we must confront this question. A good conscience carries a high premium. Its fruits are positive. Its way is expensive. Yet it produces authentic living. Why? Because it results in a consistency of life. You know you are what you claim to be. Your life becomes an open book. When there is failure, you confront it openly. The world sees. Embarrassing? Possibly. But the truth wins out. God's grace is sufficient. Your life is authentic.

2. *Think about whatever is noble.* The *King James Version* translates this as *honest.* It really means worthy of reverence. Does your thought have deep-down value? Is there dignity? Is there nobility of thought? Thoughts of God lift you up. John Calvin described the sanctity of honorable thoughts: "A virtue which

consists in our walking worthy of our vocation, keeping away from all profane filthiness" (*Calvin's Commentaries,* Eerdmans, Vol. 11, p. 290). Are you inclined to honorable living? Is there dignity in your lifestyle? Do you move through the world as if your body were a temple of God? All too often we emphasize flippancies. We lose the sense of eternal values, much to our own distress.

Imagine that today you received an invitation to address a joint session of Congress. What clothes would you wear? How would you carry yourself? What would you say? There would be a note of dignity. You would take it seriously. What a privilege! Take the life God has given you with as much seriousness and reverence. Carry yourself with honor. You are privileged to be about His business. You represent the King of kings!

3. *Think about whatever is right.* Or as the *King James Version* states it, *just.* Justice is dealing fairly with both God and fellowman. There's more to life than pleasure. Each of us must possess a sense of responsibility and be careful not to defraud or injure anyone. "Do what is right in the eyes of everybody" (Rom. 12:17).

Justice is taking another person's concerns as seriously as I do my own. I become willing to look out for his well-being, and give him every opportunity. Is what I'm doing, what I'm thinking, right? Is it fair?

4. *Think about whatever is pure.* Chastity is out of style today. Moral purity is scoffed at. Yet we who believe in Christ are called to purity.

Walking to work one morning, I observed a gang of teenagers hanging around a street corner. As I stopped for a few moments and listened to these young men, I heard foul language strong enough to burn my ears. What future do they have, bombarding their minds with impure thoughts? They encourage each other in impure actions, never stopping to ask the question, "Is it pure?"

God calls you to chastity in every aspect of your life. Is this your aspiration?

5. *Think about whatever is lovely.* This simply and clearly means *worthy of love.* Are you endeavoring to cultivate the quality of genuineness to others? What are you thinking? Is it lovely? What are

you doing? It is easy to be governed by a critical spirit. This is especially true of the religious person. It is easy to stand in judgment of others, but in the process spiritual sensitivity is squelched.

6. *Think about whatever is admirable, of good report* (KJV). There are things that most people agree should be held in honor. All of us can discover good in others. We can show appreciation. We can be fair in our evaluations. We can express these evaluations positively.

We've met people who seem so fair in everything. They don't take advantage of any other person. They don't downgrade others. They are not caught up in defensiveness, always trying to prove how good they are at the expense of others. They discover the admirable traits in those around them.

Paul concludes his admonition by stating, "If anything is excellent and praiseworthy—think about such things" (Phil. 4:8). He's appealing to you and me to live lives that are commendable to the world. Both virtue and good ethics are highly regarded in pagan thinking. Paul is not asking that we win a prize from the world, but that we live in such a way that others can see the results of the transforming power of Jesus Christ in us.

How Practical Is All This?

Theoretically, all of this sounds good. I'm sure you agree that the wrong kinds of thought-conditioning are destructive. The right kinds are constructive. But how can Paul's ideas be applied for constructive thought-conditioning?

First, through a daily devotional life. The Holy Spirit is available. So don't squeeze Him out of your life by too much activity. Though Christians are to be people of action, their best actions come out of reflection. Take time to fill your thoughts with what is true, noble, right, pure, lovely, and admirable. Take time to be alone with God. Time alone with God has a qualitative influence on the rest of your day.

There are some basic components for a vital devotional life: spend time in the Word of God and let God talk to you. Take seriously the concept of making it a significant part of your thought processes everyday.

Buy a recent translation of the Bible, if you don't have one. Many inexpensive editions are available. Read and study and memorize portions of the Bible in the language you use every day. Pick one thought for each day, whether you are reading the Bible through or reading selected portions. Grab one idea which you can hold onto throughout the entire day. Even if you forget everything else, keep repeating that message to yourself. This is the best thought-conditioning. "Thy Word have I hid in mine heart, that I might not sin against Thee" (Ps. 119:11, KJV).

The second dimension for constructive thought-conditioning is prayer. Pray about specific concerns. If you keep a list, you'll be surprised to observe how many prayers God answers. Put down a date when you start praying and also one when the answer comes.

A prayer life involves adoration of God. It includes confession of sin. Thanksgiving is an integral part of conversation with the Lord. Intercession is an exciting privilege. Nothing is more exhilarating than living life with concern for others, and sharing their specific needs in prayer. Of course, continually bring your own needs to the Lord as well.

A third dimension for constructive thought-conditioning is input. The Bible is essential reading. However, it helps to supplement your Bible reading with devotional helps. These are available from your church or Christian bookstore.

Take time for *meditation.* Silence is unnatural to our culture. Our text tells us to "think on such things." John Calvin translates the word *think* as "meditate." Schedule periods of silence to meditate over ideas of God.

A friend described to me how his life had been revolutionized by daily meditation. He tried to get to the office 30 minutes before his secretary arrived. Encouraged by his reading from the Scriptures, a time of prayer, and inspirational reading, he set aside a few minutes to simply sit silently. He said, "This is the most creative time of my entire life. It's amazing how ideas about God, myself, activities of the day, my family, my work, and the society in which I live come flooding in. How arid, how dry life gets, when there's no time for silent meditation."

Discipline Is Necessary

Are you exposing your life to positive thought-conditioning? It takes discipline to think about the topics suggested by Paul. It takes discipline to have a devotional life and schedule time for thought-conditioning. Discipline is tough.

It's not easy to do your exercises. But you feel better when your body is in good condition. It's not easy to sit down and read a significant book. But you feel refreshed and challenged when you're done.

The greatest contributions to human history have come from people who were willing to apply themselves. Are you willing? Think on God's things. Such thinking not only helps your life to be fulfilled but, as Paul states, produces peace of mind.

The Results of Good Thinking

Notice how Paul goes right into the results: "And the peace of God, which transcends all understanding, will guard our hearts and our minds in Christ Jesus" (Phil. 4:7).

Peace? Is it possible? Can it be true? Or is peace an illusion?

The Bible speaks of the yearning of the heart. God Himself confronts the conflicts of our day bringing a thrilling experience— peace.

This is the *peace of God.* It's different from the world's view. Christ said, "Peace I leave with you; My peace I give you. I do not give to you as the world gives. Do not let your hearts be troubled and do not be afraid" (John 14:27).

At the time Christ spoke these words, the classical Greek view of peace was identical to the modern definition we find in a dictionary. Peace, as defined by men and women who have not been spiritually reborn in Jesus Christ, is simply the absence of war or conflict.

The non-Christian's endeavor to achieve peace suffers from a totally unrealistic view of human nature. He chooses isolated statements from Jesus' teachings such as "turn the other cheek." His deduction is that total disarmament, an unconditional withdrawal of troops, and an abolishment of the industrial-military complex would produce peace among men.

Frenchman Henri Lardon shared with me his experiences in France prior to World War II. He described how France was caught up in a quest for peace. Workers demanded higher wages. Strikers paralyzed the nation. During this social revolution, the Germans were rearming at a rapid pace. Finally came the day of reckoning. Unimpressed by France's desire for peace, on September 3, 1939 the Nazis made their move against a nation incapable of defending itself. Within eight months France had fallen.

Peace seen simply as the absence of conflict can lead to a naive optimism. Its symbol is Prime Minister Chamberlain's pre-World War II umbrella policy. Great chaos and defeat resulted.

The peace of God is different. It is not simply the negative concept which defines peace strictly as the absence of conflict. Biblical "peace" is primarily positive. It covers every single relationship in life. It captures the Old Testament "shalom." It carries into the New Testament the concept of that ideal state of life—wholeness, well-being, harmony. It embodies a totality of life which is available when a person, or a nation, is right with God.

Biblical scholar Alan Richardson writes: "The peace of unbroken union with the Father in the midst of adversity, which is the supreme gift of Jesus to the disciples and which is to be distinguished from all forms of worldly security (John 14:17), is dependent on His final victory over the chief enemies, sin and death (John 16:33). Hence it is that after the Resurrection the Lord greets His disciples with peace and shows them the marks of the passion and passes on to them His own mission and victory over sin (John 20:19-23, 26)." From *A Theological Word Book of the Bible*, Macmillan, p. 166.

God's Gospel of peace came out of God's willingness to be expendable in the person of Jesus Christ. It came out of Christ's passion—His suffering, His death, His resurrection—providing you and me with a fullness of life, a well-being, a oneness with our Creator which is otherwise impossible.

This peace *passes all human understanding.* It is not determined by material and political circumstances. People often think that peace can be identified with material affluence or with the stability of their own political views.

Many young people do not understand this fact. During the peak of violent student demonstrations in the late '60s and early '70s, I engaged a number of young radicals in intimate discussion. One of them, a girl of 17, described her inner yearning for peace. It led to joining the Weathermen, the radical wing of Students for a Democratic Society. "It's too late to bring peace by peaceful means. America needs a revolution!" she exclaimed.

Such radical response came out of a genuine desire for peace. What these youths could not understand was that peace is forever elusive by human means.

Interestingly enough, God's peace can be present even in the heart of conflict, crisis, and deprivation. In fact, often the real quality of a person's dedication to Jesus Christ is shown not in time of plenty, but in time of want.

Nothing thrills me more than reading the letters I've received from Bernard Muindi. This black pastor from Kenya experienced the peace of God even in the midst of severe religious persecution. Bernie described sensing the presence of Christ even when his life was threatened by oath-taking terrorists.

Bishop Kivengere, who was forced to flee Uganda and who knew firsthand the atrocities of President Idi Amin Dada, could also describe the attitude of peace present among the believers of his country. Many were murdered. Many were tortured. But they would not deny their allegiance to Jesus Christ. The peace of God fortified them.

Travel to Moscow with me and meet pretty "In-Tourist" guide, Ludmela. She's one of the privileged class in a so-called "classless" Communist country. As part of the Communist party, she enjoys many privileges. But Ludmela's face is not marked with happiness. She argues by the hour, describing the accomplishments of her Socialist Republic, while her nonverbal communications reveal a high degree of unhappiness and internal conflict.

Let's move on to a Baptist church hidden away in a remote part of Moscow. There "standing room only" is the norm. Hundreds of committed Christians, at great sacrifice, are willing to meet together and sing their hymns of faith. Look into their eyes and see the peace of

God which passes all human understanding. Witness that totality of life, that wholeness, that well-being, that harmony which puts any human substitute to shame.

How God's Peace Operates

This peace of God which passes "all understanding will guard your hearts and your minds in Christ Jesus" (Phil. 4:7).

This is exciting. The *Amplified Bible* states it this way: This peace "shall garrison and mount guard over your hearts and your minds in Christ Jesus." This peace which comes through a right relationship with God and Jesus Christ is a "warrior peace." It sets up guard duty and protects you. Your whole life becomes secure. It enables you to understand the basis for living.

The peace of God helps you confront the fact of your own death with the assurance that Christ has made provision for you. You have the assurance of eternity with Him in heaven. When the Apostle Paul says that this peace shall keep your heart and mind, once again he is referring to your very being—not just your body and intellect—but all that is you.

This peace has one simple condition—the condition of trust. The previous verse read: "Do not be anxious about anything, but in everything, by prayer and petition, with thanksgiving, present your requests to God" (v. 6). God's peace releases us from anxiety. Worry accomplishes nothing and is an indication of distrust of God.

His peace is available as you purpose to live under His authority and allow His plan for your life to evolve. Learn to take everything to Him in prayer. He wants to be your Friend. He wants you to turn all your problems over to Him. Remember to maintain a spirit of thanksgiving as you make your requests known to God. Then you will experience this peace—His peace—which passes all human understanding, keeping you through Jesus Christ.

11
Concerned and Contented—Can We Be Both?

I rejoice greatly in the Lord that at last you have renewed your concern for me. Indeed, you have been concerned, but you have had no opportunity to show it. I am not saying this because I am in need, for I have learned to be content whatever the circumstances. I know what it is to be in need, and I know what it is to have plenty. I have learned the secret of being content in any and every situation, whether well fed or hungry, whether living in plenty or in want. I can do everything through Him who gives me strength (Phil. 4:10-13).

How do we deal with the problem of people in need? We watch a television program on famine. A four-year-old's emaciated body is picked up from the street. The bloated stomach looks as if its weight could break the pencil-thin arms and legs. If we don't get to the set in time to turn it off, we turn our heads. It makes us uncomfortable. We don't want to see those sights. Why? Are we guilty because we have so much? Perhaps. But more than that. Those scenes make us feel helpless.

We read of poverty in our own city. We know what's going on. Then we quit reading. When we hear sermons on social needs, we become upset. Why? Helplessness is one reason. Helplessness leads to frustration. What good does it do to hear another sermon on the subject when we can do so little about the problem? It's bigger than we are.

We become upset by sermons on social issues. What right has the preacher to stimulate our guilt when he drives a new car, lives in a fine home, enjoys three excellent meals a day? (I share these reactions with you, even though I'm the preacher! How dare I talk about social needs when I myself feel so frustrated, so guilty, so overstuffed?)

And after all, isn't a concern for bodily needs the "social gospel"? We come to church to hear about Jesus Christ and His forgiveness of our sins. We need spiritual strength to get through the next few days, not a lot of talk about the world's problems!

Christ invites you to spiritual rebirth. Your life span is 70 or 80 years. Then comes eternity. As big as this earth seems now, as huge as the universe appears, your life and mine are so short. So now is the appointed time to decide for Jesus Christ.

But once you've answered the question that Christ puts to you—"Who think you that I am?"—you're confronted by another. Your Saviour looks you in the eyes and says:

"For I was hungry and you gave Me something to eat, I was thirsty and you gave Me something to drink, I was a stranger and you invited Me in, I needed clothes and you clothed Me, I was sick and you looked after Me, I was in prison and you came to visit Me" (Matt. 25:35-36).
We respond:
"Lord, when did we see You hungry and feed You, or thirsty and give You something to drink? When did we see You a stranger and invite You in, or needing clothes and clothe You? When did we see You sick or in prison and go to visit You?"
The King will reply, "I tell you the truth, whatever you did for one of the least of these brothers of Mine, you did for Me" (Matt. 25:37-40).

Why Fear "Social Gospel"?

Why are we scared of the term "social gospel"?

It was Sunday, August 24, 1969. Several days before, the hurricane

Camille had wreaked havoc on the Gulf Coast. Hundreds of people had been killed. Homes, businesses, and lifetime savings had been wiped out in a few hours of nature's fury.

Those of us living on Key Biscayne, Florida sensed a weird empathy with the storm-ravaged residents of the Louisiana-Mississippi delta areas. Subject to hurricanes ourselves, we thanked God that we had been spared. Our session met, voting unanimously to take a special offering to help fellow believers rebuild their destroyed churches. Then I preached a sermon on our responsibilities. I'll never forget the reaction of one of the dearest members of that church. Her voice registered deep concern as she said, "This morning you preached the social gospel. I warn you, that message will destroy this church!"

Did she have a legitimate concern? Possibly. There is always a danger of social concerns pushing spiritual considerations out of the way. Why? Because it's easier to concentrate on the here and now than on the eternal. You can touch objects. Spiritual concerns elude physical grasps. The emphasis on the life-changing power of Jesus Christ can quickly change to talk about love and service for others. Ethical humanism is good, but it's not good enough *for* salvation. It can be an outgrowth *of* salvation.

Yes, there are reasons to be concerned about the "social gospel." This is especially true in the United States. Toward the latter part of the 19th century and the first part of the 20th, German higher biblical criticism made inroads into American theology. The Bible, always questioned by some, came under intense, skeptical scrutiny. The historical understanding that the Bible was God's infallible self-disclosure became suspect. The seriousness of sin was minimized, the supernatural ridiculed. As a result, today we find many theologians, ministers, and Christian laymen who deny the historic verities of the Christian faith. But they are wrong. Without these and other doctrinal essentials, there is no Christian faith. There is no Gospel. There is no Good News.

Being scared of the social gospel has some merit. If it becomes the entire message of the church, Christianity is dead. It is nothing more than warmed-over, ethical humanism. If it becomes a substitute for saving faith in Jesus Christ, we should close up our buildings, or rename ourselves as social agencies.

The Biblical Approach

What does the Bible say about the social gospel? Frankly, it doesn't allow this division between spiritual and social concerns. We haven't the option to declare, "We'll talk about the spiritual," or "We'll talk about the social." Either one expressed to the exclusion of the other is heresy. The vertical break of God into human history intersects with our responsibilities to our fellowman. It intersects at the cross of Jesus Christ.

> One day they tried to back Jesus to the wall with the question, "Teacher, which is the great commandment in the Law?"
> Jesus replied, "Love the Lord your God with all your heart and with all your soul and with all your mind." This is the first and greatest commandment. And the second is like it: "Love your neighbor as yourself. All the Law and the Prophets hang on these two commandments" (Matt. 22:36-40).

There it is. The vertical relationship. The horizontal relationship. Sprinkled all through the Scriptures are both calls—to trust the Lord and to serve mankind. You could spend the next few months going through the Scriptures, underlining in one color all references dealing with your relationship to the Lord, and then underlining in another color all those dealing with your horizontal responsibilities, man to man. You'd be amazed to discover how frequent the references are to the needy. The Jewish people took their poor seriously. Frequent offerings were received for the poor in both money and goods. The early church carried out those same responsibilities. Christianity is wholistic. Christ deals with the whole person. He's interested in soul *and* body. He calls His church to minister both to the souls and the bodies of others.

Of the Ten Commandments, the first four deal with God-oriented responsibilities. The last six deal with relationships with other human beings. God help us to bring together the spiritual and the social dimensions of the Gospel of Jesus Christ.

Opportunity

It all becomes a matter of *opportunity*. There was Paul in prison. He wrote to his friends at Philippi: "I rejoice greatly in the Lord that at last you have renewed your concern for me. Indeed, you have been concerned, but you had no opportunity to show it" (Phil. 4:10).

Paul had just received some financial help from the Philippians. He mentioned their gifts brought by Epaphroditus. The words he used probed at two points. One, he reminded his brothers and sisters to be revived in their concern for others. John Calvin writes about it this way: "He rejoiced that they had gained new vigor so as to exercise care for him." This metaphor is taken from the trees. There is a strength which, drawn inward, begins to flourish again in the spring. Apparently the Philippian church had been dormant. Now they were revived in their interests. Then Paul added a second dimension. Instead of chiding them for not having been of more help, he noted their difficulties. Recognizing that now their circumstances had improved to the point where they could help again, he thanked them for acting on their new opportunity.

Three specific definitions of opportunity show aspects of Christian social concern. One is *attitude*. Paul says, "At last you have renewed your concern for me." So often our concerns are directed inward. We become protective of our own interests. So few of our concerns are outgoing.

The second definition of opportunity is that of *resources*. What are our resources and what are we doing with them? Some of us are wealthy by the world's standards. How do we hold onto our possessions? I heard Anglican Bishop Alfred Stanway of Australia say it this way, "Hold your possessions on the open palm of your hand. That way it is less painful than if your hand is clenched and God wants to take some of them." How willing are we to let our material possessions be expendable?

Some don't have much in the way of material resources. But they have time. They have energy. They have abilities. They can work to help others who are in need. This becomes their opportunity and their joy.

A third definition of opportunity is the privilege of *selectivity*. We personally can't solve all the world's problems. That's why we're tempted to do nothing. The Philippian church didn't help everybody. To have done that would have been to spread too thin the concentrated help made possible by selective giving. We can't do everything. But we need to open our hearts to those opportunities in which we have the ability to help.

Real evangelical concern revolutionizes both the lives of individuals and society. God's view is that the Gospel is both personal and social.

What Can I Do?

You can ask God to bring into your life someone who has deep personal, spiritual, or physical needs. You can be that person's minister. You can help a sick and alone person get back and forth to a hospital. You can supply a present need of someone in poverty. You can become a friend to the friendless.

Try the experiment of one group who decided to live within a poverty budget for a month. After one family did this, the father described his experience: "I didn't know how secure money can make you feel. It was necessary for me to spend some days away from home on business. To stay on the poverty allotment, I had to search stores for the best food deals; I had to live in charity organization accommodations. I had to eat in my car. I drove to a less congested area of the parking lot and began to eat my bread and other cheaper foods. I was glad I didn't have to share with anyone. My lifestyle had been that of self-satisfaction and bodily comforts. This poverty budget brought me to a painful realization. Thinking of Christ's call for the discipline to follow Him filled me with shame for my selfishness and compassion for those living at the poverty level continually."

No, you can't do everything. But you can do something to touch the personal and social needs of those around you. If each one reading this message would take on one personal project of overt love and caring, his city and his world would be in a lot better shape. "Forgive me, O God, for not doing a better job of practicing what I preach."

Have True Contentment

Having everything isn't the secret of contentment. Many who live in poverty seem to be far more contented than the rich. In fact, middle-class Americans and rich Americans seem to be the most restless. Many of them haven't caught the spirit of the apostle, who had "learned to be content whatever the circumstances" (Phil. 4:11).

Are you caught up in this restlessness? Does home life no longer satisfy? Does your job provide a living—but that's about all? Do you feel hemmed in by responsibilities? If so, contentment doesn't describe your situation.

What a rat race! Sadly enough, many Christians are caught up in this restlessness. They are discontented.

What Is Contentment?

Contentment is a *kind of self-sufficiency*. It is not based on outward circumstances. Take the Apostle Paul, an excellent example. He was financially insolvent. He had just received a gift from the church at Philippi. He wrote back expressing appreciation for the money, but added that he had learned how to live without it as well as with it. As much as he appreciated his few material possessions, he wanted to make it clear that he was financially "riding loose in the saddle." In effect, he was saying, "Contentment goes beyond financial security. There's an internal quality, a serenity, which goes beyond outward circumstances. One can be up or down in finances, romance, health, friendships, and still have the stabilizing influence of a contented outlook. External security is not for a moment synonymous with contentment."

Contentment is not a state of life in which you are propped up by artificial protections. It is not a security which assures that you will not be buffeted by ups and downs.

Instead, contentment is that inner sense of self-sufficiency which says, "No matter what comes along, I have the capacity to meet it head-on. Whether it be joy or sorrow, sickness or health, plenty or want, I will continue. I have the inner resources. I have an inner fullness of life."

Contentment is something which is *learned*. It does not happen overnight. Paul says, "For I have *learned* to be content whatever the circumstances." He says, "I *know* what it is to be in need, and I know what it is to have plenty. I have learned the secret of being content in any and every situation."

One translation of these words from the Greek is, "I have found the secret of life." Yet another says, "I have been initiated through the experience of life to know how to be content." This is Paul, the veteran, speaking. This man has been around. He says, "I can bear any extremes. I can get good out of the ups and downs. When I have an empty, hungry stomach, I learn what it feels like to be without. Through this, there comes a new discipline of body and mind. When I have a full stomach, I realize how much I have to be thankful for. When I look back over life, I see that somehow I've been brought through all this and I have learned much."

If you are living a life which is not content, you need to learn greater lessons in the schoolhouse of faith. Look to the past. Has God ever let you down? You've had your difficult times. You've had your heartbreaks. You're still living with some of them. But have you ever found God wanting? Has God neglected you when the chips were down? Survey the history of your Christian commitment. I think you'll be amazed to see that somehow, at every point in crisis, God stood by you.

The Source of Contentment and Strength

Paul says, "I have learned to be content whatever the circumstances" (Phil. 4:11), because this contentment wasn't the product of any Stoic fatalism but rather the product of an active, dynamic reliance on Jesus Christ. He says, "I can do everything through Him who gives me strength" (Phil. 4:13).

There is a Source of strength outside yourself which can develop your self-sufficiency. Both the Christian and the non-Christian have their ups and downs. But a godless life has weakness at its base. True contentment is the capacity to live realistically in the present, based on a personal relationship with Jesus Christ.

This in essence is *risky living.* Christ calls you to expendability. Management consultant Peter Drucker describes four kinds of risks:

the first one—you must accept; the second—you can afford to take; the third—you cannot afford to take; the fourth one—you cannot afford not to take. Paul was willing to risk his safety and sacrifice his comfort for the sake of Jesus Christ. No cost was too great to hold him back in his evangelistic efforts. He saw Christian living as being a risk he could not afford *not* to take. He had to follow his Lord.

In the process, Paul uncovered an exciting principle. You are not really a free person until you are willing to lose everything. There is no true contentment until you have been set free from the bondage of your possessions, your status, your reputation, your goals.

Jesus Christ was free to purchase your salvation. He now sets you free to high-risk living, which doesn't depend on artificial props.

Some Christians are restless, lacking the capacity of living lives of contentment in the present tense. They spend much of their lives looking back to days more pleasant than the present. Some also live in continual anticipation of the future. Anxiously they await the day when all will be better than it is in the present. They would give anything for the future to come. Are you discontented trying to get ahead of God? When discontented with the present and anxious about the future, remember: Your life is in Christ. He strengthens you. He upholds His plan for your life.

Live your life now, in faith. Live it to the fullest, no matter what your frustrations may be. Don't allow yourself to move ahead of God. Learn to live in the dimension of contentment which says, "For I have learned to be content whatever the circumstances." Then you'll discover some of the greatest ways to become a concerned person. The contented person is free to become concerned about social needs near and far. He has absolute confidence in God to keep him while he ministers to the needy. Contentment and concern—both are possible —both are necessary to fulfill the desire of Christ for your life.

12
Having Our
Needs Supplied

Yet it was good of you to share in my troubles. Moreover, as you Philippians know, in the early days of your acquaintance with the Gospel, when I set out from Macedonia, not one church shared with me in the matter of giving and receiving, except you only; for even when I was in Thessalonica, you sent me aid again and again when I was in need. Not that I am looking for a gift, but I am looking for what may be credited to your account. I have received full payment and even more; I am amply supplied, now that I have received from Epaphroditus the gifts you sent. They are a fragrant offering, an acceptable sacrifice, pleasing to God. And my God will meet all your needs according to His glorious riches in Christ Jesus (Phil. 4:14-19).

Paying so much attention to the provisions given to him by the Philippians even after declaring, "I can do everything through Him who gives me strength" (v. 13), and "I have learned the secret of being content in any and every situation" (v. 12) wasn't an incongruity in Paul's thinking. It simply showed the appreciation he had for their kindnesses. It also indicated the strong connection Paul made between faith and practice. His former co-workers' generosity could be expected. If they hadn't sacrificially reached out to supply his needs, he would have been rightfully surprised.

So, after being thankful for their provision to him, Paul confidently declared, "My God will meet all your needs according to His glorious riches in Christ Jesus" (v. 19).

Is this some naive optimism? I can't think of a better thought-conditioner than this positive affirmation of confidence. This is not simply the kind of "buck up, old chap" attitude presented in so much of the modern literature of our day. Paul had hope because he had Christ.

The Gospel of Jesus Christ challenges us to positive thinking. Yet this Christian style of living which is marked by buoyant optimism has its feet firmly on the ground. Paul was not playing games with himself when he penned the words, "My God will meet all your needs according to His glorious riches in Christ Jesus." He knew what it was to suffer. He stated, "I know what it is to be in need, and I know what it is to have plenty. I have learned the secret of being content in any and every situation, whether well fed or hungry, whether living in plenty or in want" (v. 12).

Out of this context he made the optimistic statement, "I can do everything through Him who gives me strength" (v. 13).

I am sure Paul sensed the inevitable death which awaited him. He was to die a martyr for his faith. No head-in-the-clouds spirit undergirded his words of confidence. They came from a man who had suffered, he was speaking to people who would face great difficulties. God's promise still stands. We can grab hold of it too. Nothing is too hard for Him.

The Source of Supply

There is One who can meet our every need. His name is Jesus Christ.

Many people sense a divine personality which brought this world into being. Paul adds an additional dimension to the eternal human confidence that there is some force outside ourselves. He says: "*My* God will meet all your needs" (v. 19, author's italics). This interjects a highly personal possessive pronoun which describes man's relationship with Almighty God—"*My* God."

The promises of the Bible are not for everyone. Paul made it clear they can only be appropriated by obedient Christians.

A Covenant Relationship

We cannot claim God's provision for all we need if we are not recipients of His greatest provision—salvation. God is not our God if we are not personally related to Him through Jesus Christ. *"My* God" implies that I have certain rights to Him. He is mine. He has identified with me to the point that I can claim Him as my own.

My wife is mine in a highly unique way. True, she maintains an identity of her own. She has her own ego, personality, strengths, and weaknesses. She functions independently of me. At the same time, she is mine. She has chosen to enter into the intimate relationship of marriage to the point where she allows me to call her mine. And I allow her to claim a personal access to me. I am hers in the same way that she is mine.

My daughters are also mine. Granted, the day will probably come when each will choose another man. Yet as long as I live, they will be mine in a personal and biological relationship. I have a right to them.

My right to my wife Anne is based on covenant, on contract. My right to my daughters is based on blood relationship. They will always be a part of me.

You have a right to God if you receive Him. He has made Himself available to you. Your access is one of covenant, of contract. It is also one of birthright: "To all who received Him, to those who believed in His name, He gave the right to become children of God" (John 1:12). God doesn't scatter His promises helter-skelter. They are given only to those who have acknowledged Jesus Christ as Saviour and Lord.

This promise is not even given to all Christians. Not every Christian can claim God's full provision. The promises of God's Word are based on obedience. His promises are based on being a responsible steward of God's grace. I personally don't believe you can lose your salvation once you have authentically come to Christ through repentance and faith. However, you can lose God's favor and power in your life. You can short-circuit the power line of provision which God has for you.

Jesus talked about talents. One man was given 10, another 5, another 1. Each had been instructed to use his talents to the fullest as a good steward of God's provisions. Two were congratulated for their faithfulness. The other had his talent taken away because he was irresponsible.

God has gifted you. If you are a responsible steward of what He has given to you, you will realize His richest blessing. God wants your obedience.

A disobedient child often loses things which would otherwise be available. I remember the most poignant experience I had along this line. In 1952, as a 12-year-old, I qualified for a scholarship at a fine New England prep school, Belmont Hill. Within walking distance of my home, this school provided excellent training. Many of its graduates went on to Harvard and other Ivy League schools. Belmont Hill also had a superior sports program. I loved to play hockey and aspired to be on that team. My parents were thrilled with the idea. As a minister, Dad could not afford to send me. But the scholarship made this possible.

During that summer of 1952, I became a bit difficult for my parents to handle—a better term—disobedient! I did things they told me not to do. I didn't do things they requested. Finally, they informed me that if I continued, I would not have the privilege of going to Belmont Hill. I didn't believe their threat.

One day at our summer place in Indiana I got into a boat and headed off across the lake. This was in direct disobedience to my father. With me was a 15-year-old blonde waitress who had been placed on my parents' unacceptable list. My parents caught me. Much to my amazement, they stood by their word, "No Belmont Hill!" You may think this was a bit harsh. But I caught on to the fact that Mom and Dad were serious. Because they loved me, they wanted me to learn obedience. No amount of cajoling or promising on my part caused them to reverse their decision. I continued on in the public school system. I never did go to Belmont Hill.

The person who lives appropriating the fullest provision of God's promises is following Jesus Christ. He lives in obedience to the will of God as revealed in the Scriptures. He can't cut corners with God and claim His fullest blessing. A check of every person in the Bible will reveal how tragedy resulted from disobedience. God provided blessings to those who lived in conformity to His will.

The God of provision, the Creator-Sustainer God of all human history, is or can be yours through Jesus Christ. The God of grace, who became a man to die for your sins and rise in resurrection power, is or can be your God. He is the Source of supply for every need you have. Praise God from whom all blessings flow!

Supply for All Your "Needs"

Do you know your needs, both spiritual and material? There is a source of supply *for your needs*... all of them. It's according to God's riches in glory by Christ Jesus.

The gasoline service station where you trade is a supplier. He supplies gas for your car. He supplies a checkup on your engine. Perhaps he also makes various other services available. Imagine the inconvenience if 90 percent of the service stations evaporated. Sometimes you would have no provision for your car. What you take for granted—it's right down the block now—would become a commodity for which you'd have to travel many miles. You got this feeling during recent fuel shortages. No longer did you take your supplier for granted.

Your local druggist has many suppliers. He has a candy supplier. He has a drug supplier. He has a magazine supplier. He has a newspaper supplier. He has a cosmetics supplier. Cut off the sources of supply and he'd either have to reorganize or cease his whole business. It's impossible to stock up just once for all time. There's a constant need for resupplying stock and getting in new products.

God wants to be your continual Supplier. Your God—the One with whom you have a personal relationship—is interested in you. He doesn't simply convert you and leave you. He wants to be the continuing energizing Provider of all your needs.

If you depend on Him, God will supply *all* your needs. The Bible doesn't say some of them. It says *all* of them. It doesn't say that God is interested in you only as a spiritual entity, that He just wants to save your soul and let the world ravage you mentally, socially, and physically. God is interested in every detail of your life. *All* is a small word but is the ultimate in relation to quantity. *"My* God" is a pretty big God!

Now, let's remember that *all of our wants aren't needs*. For instance, we have a tendency toward gluttony. We want more than is essential.

I was at a birthday party. In the center of one room was a pinata. Youngsters were swinging sticks at it. Finally the bag burst and candy flew all over the room. Adults stood by laughing as the youngsters scrambled for the pieces of candy. One child began crying when his parents insisted that, since he was the biggest and had grabbed the most, he should share some of it with the smaller children. That was difficult for him—just as it is difficult for us to admit that we don't need everything we grasp for or attain. After all, when we work hard for something don't we deserve to keep it?

God is interested in the smallest details of life. He will meet our every need if we are believers committed to Jesus Christ. Yet He also has the capacity to differentiate between what we need and what we think we need. Alexander Maclaren states it this way: "If we do not get what we want, we may be quite sure that we do not need it."

Jesus Christ is central to all of this: "And My God will meet all your needs according to His glorious riches in Christ Jesus" (Phil. 4:19).

The Apostle Paul says that everything is in Christ. Christ is all. The man who has Christ has all things. "All are yours, and ye are Christ's; and Christ is God's" (1 Cor. 3:22-23, KJV). If you trust Christ all your needs will be supplied in and by Him. If you need courage to live in these tough, contemporary times, He can provide it. If you need patience in impossible situations, He can provide it. If you need love, Jesus Christ can give it to you. If you need forgiveness for sins, He's able to wash you white as snow and make you just as if you had never sinned. Supplying everything you need is based on His being God. It is in the miracle of God-become-man that all of your needs are met.

The most cataclysmic event of all human history up to this point was the coming of Christ—to meet your deepest needs. The most cataclysmic event of all human history yet to happen will be the Second Coming of Jesus Christ—to consummate God's plan for this world. "The Lord is my Shepherd, I shall lack nothing" (Ps. 23:1). This is the posture of the believer who puts his faith and trust in Jesus Christ.

Present Your Needs to Him

Come with your personal needs. Your body—is it broken? Is it weary? He can bring healing. Perhaps this will be literal, for many have sensed His touch that has wiped away physical infirmities. If not that, He'll bring the healing touch that gives the capacity to live within the limitations of your problems. Your soul can be touched by God's Spirit. Like the old Gospel song says, "Are you tired and heavy-laden, cumbered with a load of care?" Come to Jesus. He'll meet your need. Bring to Him your personal problems, and the problems of your family. Bring to Him the cares of the present. Bring to Him the anxieties of the future. Bring to Him your needs in this life—and for the life to come. Jesus Christ deals in both time and eternity. "My God will meet all your needs" (Phil. 4:19).

I have needs, so many I could not relate them all. I have needs as a man. I have needs as a husband. I have needs as a father. I have needs as a neighbor. I have needs as a citizen. I have needs as a pastor. But, thank God, provision is available for *all* my needs, not just some of them. My joy is to claim this provision as a believer in Christ endeavoring to be obedient to the will of God.

Imagine all of our needs piled together—millions of Christians with multiplied needs. We're to bring them all to Jesus Christ, and leave them with Him. We are not to bring them to Him and then take them back to ourselves.

As you go on in life, as you mature in your Christian development and outreach, your needs increase. They don't decrease. You need constant daily provision. Perhaps you need patience to live in an impossible situation. You need fresh patience for today. You can't depend on yesterday's supply, nor does the Lord want you to. He supplies your needs on a day-to-day basis—with the same power and concern that He always shows when you present your needs to Him.

Charles Haddon Spurgeon said, "Old patience is stale stuff" *(The Treasury of the Bible,* vol. 3, p. 549). Yesterday's supply isn't sufficient for today. You need a fresh supply. But that's the way it is with God. He supplies on a daily basis. Talk over today's needs today.

Also come with the needs of others. Jesus wants you to be His vehicle of outreach. It's a great spiritual principle—to bear another's burdens—plug into another, not trying to go it alone in this world. Much of the suffering of St. Paul came directly from the fact that he was willing to count it all joy to suffer for Christ, knowing that his God would meet the deepest need of others through his faithfulness. His promise to the Philippian Christians was partially based on their willingness to share with him.

There are other needs—needs of people everywhere to know of Christ. As you reach out to others, you develop a greater capacity to receive from God.

The best way to kill your own effectiveness and joy is to be so caught up in your own needs that you have no sensitivity to the person sitting next to you. That person too is a bundle of needs. Come to Christ for the provision to meet the needs of that person. My God will supply every need of yours—of mine—and of others—according to His glorious riches in Christ Jesus.

13
Values of Expanding Christian Fellowship

Greet all the saints in Christ Jesus. The brothers who are with me send greetings. All the saints send you greetings, especially those who belong to Caesar's household.

The grace of the Lord Jesus Christ be with your spirit (Phil. 4:21-23).

Paul's final words to the Philippian church are hauntingly fascinating. The more I ponder this fourth chapter, the more I realize the substantial, ongoing message related here: the evidence of a depth of Christian relationship between believers whether they were near or far.

These somewhat commonplace words of blessing, salutation, and benediction bring to mind other biblical verses which talk about the nature of the Christian church. These words paint a picture of a body which is called the church. Every member of that body fits into its unique place as essential to the overall function of the church. This biblical imagery is ingrained in my mind.

My curiosity has been aroused by the title of one of Dr. Ray C. Stedman's books, *Body Life* (Regal Books Div., G/L Publications). For several years it had gathered dust on my bookshelf until I pulled it down. Then I devoured each page with an insatiable hunger, whetted by my own need to learn more about the relationships of believers in the broad worldwide context of the church.

Perhaps of greater significance was the stimulation Anne and I have received in making moves from Key Biscayne, Florida to Pittsburgh, Pennsylvania, and now to Newport Beach, California. Frankly, it's somewhat humbling to learn from one's successors. When I left these two pastorates I wanted to think that God had moved me to bigger and better ministries. Instead, I'm becoming more and more convinced that in His strategy He removed me from my former charges so that new and exciting ministries could take place through the gifts of others. At the same time, I know that He brought me to my present ministry to help lead others into new dimensions of spiritual service.

Exciting Community

Paul had his problems. Who doesn't? But it's one thing to handle one's problems all alone; it's another thing to be involved in dynamic, human, spiritual relationships. Paul was energized spiritually, both by the presence of God's Holy Spirit in his life and by the community of fellow believers he found wherever he went. Paul was part of a divine human organism bigger than himself. Its name—the church.

Granted, churches have their problems too. Just as families have their squabbles, so there are squabbles within local churches. Just as families have financial problems, so do churches. Any basic problems we have in the 20th century can be matched by those of the first century church. Within several decades of the time Christ founded His church, He found it necessary to reveal to the Apostle John His message to the churches of Asia Minor. Christ drew attention to their slippages back to lukewarmness, lack of faith, immorality, heresy, and lovelessness. And He called them back to be vital communities. (See Rev. 1—3.)

Some Family Words

The believers at Philippi were not perfect. Paul exhorted them to deeper faith. He urged them to claim the promises of God. He rebuked. But his final words were family words.

He addressed words of blessing to God: "To our God and Father be glory for ever and ever. Amen" (Phil. 4:20). He made this ascription of praise, acknowledging the glory of God the Father.

Then he moved from this vertical upthrust to a horizontal outreach. He expressed his salutation, greeting every saint in Christ Jesus. The isolated apostle urged the leaders of the Philippian church to give his regards to all the fellow believers at Philippi. He paused for a moment, remembering that he was writing from a local congregation at Rome to another local congregation at Philippi. His brother Christians in the capital city were aware of their linkage with fellow believers in northern Greece. He said, "The brothers who are with me send greetings. All the saints send you greetings, especially those who belong to Caesar's household" (Phil. 4:21-22).

Paul referred to his fellow Christians as "saints." They were linked together by the vertical encounter they had had with the living God through Jesus Christ. He did not imply that they were a group of faultless other-worldly angels. He identified them quite differently— as men and women redeemed by the grace of our Lord Jesus Christ.

He talked in family terms. These saints were "brothers." They had a blood relationship—that blood was shed by their Lord. They were His adopted sons and daughters. They were part of His family. This human horizontal linkage was made possible by Christ's work on the cross.

Paul's reference to "those who belong to Caesar's household" is fascinating. Here was a unique linkage of two groups of people who had nothing in common but Christ. Roman functionaries, part of Nero's retinue, were a different breed from the Macedonian Greeks. But they had a mutual concern. They possessed a oneness which came through Jesus Christ. A living dynamic crossed external barriers, bringing a family relationship among believers in one part of the world with those in another. Today we could travel to almost any country on earth and find an immediate, personal, family identity with brother and sister Christians. There would be immediate rapport between fellow saints in America and those in Kenya, or in the mountains of Formosa, or in the jungles of Ecuador, or in the throbbing cities of India, Japan, or Germany.

No Boundaries in God's Family

The Gospel of Jesus Christ knows no exclusivity. It penetrates impossible situations. It does not separate people by denominations. It is not limited by nationalities or skin color. It isn't limited to any particular economic stratum of society.

In Paul's day, this underground movement of the church made its way right into the emperor's palace. His mercy broke into what John Calvin calls "that sink of all crimes and iniquities" *(Calvin's Commentaries,* Eerdmans, Vol. 11, p. 295), the corrupt palace of the Roman emperor. A wonderful holiness reigned in the lives of some of those civil servants, making them one in Christ with Paul and with believers at Philippi.

A pious environment is not necessary. Jesus Christ can rule over the most incredible situations. You need not find yourself blocked off from fellow Christians or from Christ by any human barriers. There's no condition over which Jesus Christ cannot triumph.

A Benediction

Paul concludes his letter with words of benediction. "The grace of the Lord Jesus Christ be with your spirit" (Phil. 4:23). Grace. What is it? It's the unmerited favor of God which caught hold of Paul on the road to Damascus, transforming his life. Paul sends only one gift to his Philippian fellow saints. It's a blessing—a benediction—a prayer that God's continuing, unmerited favor will stand by them, protecting the family God has created. God's grace enables you and me to cope with life. It keeps us linked together in a mutuality of experience better and bigger than our own isolated, single parts.

Growing Together

These final words of Paul trigger a transition to the biblical concept of "Christian body life." We are not alone. Our Sunday worship dare not be merely a brief encounter between God and solitary worshipers, preacher and congregation. Instead, it is symbolic of God's family gathered together from various workaday experiences. In worship you and I engage in a family reunion. We are a body. If we know Jesus Christ personally, we are inextricably connected to the person who sits beside us, who also shares faith in Jesus Christ.

You are instructed to grow up together, even as the body develops through the maturation process. Paul writes to the church at Ephesus: "Speaking the truth in love, we will in all things grow up into Him who is the Head, that is, Christ. From Him the whole body, joined and held together by every supporting ligament, grows and builds itself up in love, as each part does its work" (Eph. 4:15-16).

We are members of His body (Eph. 5:30). To the Corinthian church Paul expressed these words: "Now you are the body of Christ, and each one of you are a part of it" (1 Cor. 12:27).

Do you catch the excitement in the implications of this body life? Each of us is interconnected. Each of us has goals and our jobs to do. The church of Jesus Christ is not a physical building. It is not a dues-paying organization. It is not a club where religious language is used instead of fraternal handshakes. The church is a dynamic organism made up of single cells which are interdependent on each other for survival.

Spiritual Gifts

In the process, God gives you two special spiritual gifts. One is the gift of *spiritual grace*. This is your *salvation*. This is that unmerited favor which God manifests in accepting you. The second is His gift of *special grace*. He takes you—a person who has experienced His spiritual grace—and gives you the *equipment* to serve Jesus Christ, empowered by His resurrection.

Let's look at this another way. First God provides redemption by His grace—forgiving you of sin, presenting you with a new start. Then, as a new person in Jesus Christ, you are entrusted with the responsibility of service. He puts you to work. In fact, you are a minister in His church. You are responsible for doing His work here on earth and using His gift of special grace.

But you say, "That doesn't make sense. I'm just a layman. I haven't any special schooling. I can't be a minister." If you're a Christian, you're a minister, whether you realize it or not.

The Bible makes a special distinction in gifts. On the one hand there are the *supportive gifts,* which are given to those of us who are set aside for special ministries, such as preaching and teaching. Paul declared, "It was He who gave some to be apostles, some to be prophets, some to be evangelists, and some to be pastors and teachers, to prepare God's people for works of service, so that the body of Christ may be built up" (Eph. 4:11-12). This means those of us serving on the church staff may have been misnamed. We are not ministers. We are the enablers. We are the equippers who are trusted with the responsibility of helping you carry out your ministry. We should be called pastors. You are the ministers.

Remember the final years of Bill Russell's job with the Boston Celtics? He became a "player-coach." He instructed his fellow players and was paid by the management to help them win games. Not only did he have a leadership responsibility; he remained a player. His instruction was enhanced by his own experience. He was not allowed the luxury of pontificating from above in the front office. Fellow players knew that he was one of them. He worked out until his muscles ached just as theirs did. He was the leader. He was the coach. He was responsible to share with them at their points of pain, discipline, and strategy. Yet his own playing of the game could not get in the way of their playing. He would fail in his responsibility if he could not help them work together as a team. He couldn't be the only star. He had to bring out the best in all the other basketball players.

There are direct parallels in this story to our being workers in the church. Pastors are to be player-coaches, helping the members succeed in the tasks God has assigned to them. Pastors are gifts of support to believers to help them use their gifts of service.

Every one of us has a different gift or gifts. Each of us is essential to the body of Christ. You have the exciting potential to minister in the name of Jesus Christ. You are part of this body in that if you hurt, I hurt. If I hurt, you hurt. The body's maimed if it has no hands. Perhaps you are one of the hands of Christ's body. The body becomes lopsided if it is missing any part.

We've all seen someone who is an amputee. The remaining parts of the amputee's body have to work overtime to compensate for the missing part. How marvelous if all the parts of His body would function together in perfect harmony.

What happens when we discover this body-life concept. We, as individual ministers, break out of the walls of the church. We scatter through our communities and world, refreshed for greater acts of service. We come together to learn more about our wonderful Lord Jesus. However, our evangelism does not go on primarily within the walls of our meeting place. It goes on where we work. In our homes. In our social relationships.

We are ministers of Christ, gifted in our acts of service reflecting His power at every point to which He deploys us. God has a strategy. We are a part of it. He has placed us where we are for a reason. There is no accident in His planning.

As this body-life principle has developed at the Peninsula Bible Church in Palo Alto, California, two kinds of business have been transacted within the church walls. One is that of the proclamation of the Word of God. The other is that of fellowship.

The body comes together to hear what God has to say. It is instructed. It is encouraged. It is rebuked. Not only does it gather for instruction—it gathers to find common refreshment. Then there is fellowship. There is the sharing of hurts as well as joys. There is the testimony of failure as well as victory. There is the sharing of needs as well as reports of God's provision. The church finds in its gathered form, teaching and refreshment. In this relaxed atmosphere ministers report their experiences. Then all are able to bear one another's burdens. Then all go forth to do the works of service.

If you aren't aware of them, I hope you will pray that God will reveal what special gifts He has given you. He has a job for you to do. He wants to help you. Together with other believers, you can seek His will in discovering your gifts.

This has been a challenge to me—to discover the body life of the church. It is the purpose for which the church exists; to discover one's gifts; to share each other's burdens; to enable each other in mutual ministries.

This concept of church body life gives a new perspective of what the church of Jesus Christ is all about. All of us, with our own gifts, are essential to bodily wholeness. And as we express our gifts—and allow others to express theirs—we discover a oneness with believers wherever we go, regardless of their denominational name or economic status. To all such believers we have an immediate affiliation, and should express our most sincere and tender love. May the grace of our Lord Jesus Christ be with you, and with all believers wherever they go. Then we'll know in an exciting and dynamic way that His grace, mercy, love and power are with us all.